THE
ANALYTICAL
MARKETER

THE
ANALYTICAL
MARKETER

HOW TO TRANSFORM
YOUR MARKETING ORGANIZATION

● ● ● ● ●

ADELE SWEETWOOD

HARVARD BUSINESS REVIEW PRESS

BOSTON, MASSACHUSETTS

The web addresses referenced in this book were live and correct at the time of the book's publication but may be subject to change.

Library of Congress Cataloging-in-Publication Data

Names: Sweetwood, Adele, author.
Title: The analytical marketer : how to transform your marketing organization / Adele Sweetwood.
Description: Boston, Massachusetts: Harvard Business Review Press, [2016]
Identifiers: LCCN 2016016047 | ISBN 9781625278456 (hardcover : alk. paper)
Subjects: LCSH: Marketing—Technological innovations. | Marketing—Management. | Quantitative research.
Classification: LCC HF5415.13 .S996 2016 | DDC 658.8/02—dc23
LC record available at https://lccn.loc.gov/2016016047

ISBN: 9781625278456
eISBN: 9781625278463

The paper used in this publication meets the requirements of the American National Standard for Permanence of Paper for Publications and Documents in Libraries and Archives Z39.48-1992.

This story would not have come to life without the people of SAS Americas Marketing & Support, more affectionately known as SAMS. This book is for and about SAMS, the organization that provided me with some of the most enriching experiences of my career.

I dedicate this book to SAMS—for always being present, for choosing the best attitude, for creating fun at work, and for making my day, every day.

CONTENTS

FOREWORD

This excellent book is a clear-eyed, down-to-earth chronicle of one of the most significant changes taking place in business today—the transformation of the marketing function.

The stereotype—and, to some degree, the reality—of marketing in the latter half of the twentieth century is made clear in one of my favorite *Dilbert* cartoons. Dilbert looks with longing at a party the marketers are having (clearly, as an engineer, he hasn't been invited). Over the entrance to the party is a banner: "Welcome to Marketing! Two drink minimum." Marketers were creative, improvisational, subjective, artistic, and (sometimes overly) sociable. Their focus was on persuading people to adopt products and services through advertising and promotions. Company outsiders in ad agencies and PR firms did much of the best work in the function. Since no one could measure the influence of print and TV advertising on sales, success was measured by industry awards rather than any financial results.

This picture began to change when direct mail and customer databases made some inroads into measurement and attribution in the latter decades of that century. However, the real revolution got underway with the Internet and World Wide Web around the turn of the twenty-first century. These technologies involved "addressability," in that firms could know who they were addressing with marketing activities and what behaviors followed. For the first time, companies could extensively measure advertising, promotions, and marketing-oriented content—whether and how long recipients viewed them and what they did after. Because marketers could know who actually bought their products and services, they could do a much more effective job of qualifying leads. And that meant that they could and needed to work more closely with the sales function. In a decade or less, marketing functions could change their entire way of working and destroy old stereotypes.

And while marketers may be familiar with this transition at a general level, implementing this change in your own marketing organization is difficult and takes time. It's very useful to have a guide, to see this transition in detail, showing what works and what doesn't, within one organization that has been on the journey of change. In many respects, although the author references a handful of leading companies making the change, this book is an extended case study of the transformation of marketing at one company, SAS. As a result, the reader can learn the context behind the general changes in marketing. What, for example, does it mean to get executive buy-in for this transformation? What new roles and structures are needed? How will these activities affect marketing budgets? How does the culture of marketing get changed over time? All these topics are treated extensively in the book and provide a template for how other organizations might undergo similar changes.

While this story is about marketing at a vendor of analytics software, there are no aspects of the transformation of marketing at SAS that another company couldn't achieve. SAS does offer some of the software described (at a high level) in these pages, but certainly not all of it. No one would mistake this book for marketing messages about SAS software. The focus is on how to use data and analytics to market in a new way, and on the needed technical capabilities.

SAS is a software company, but that does not necessarily make it easier to undergo the type of transformation I've been describing. Some aspects of marketing transformation are even more difficult at SAS than at other types of firms. Specifically, that SAS's customers are primarily businesses makes customer analytics more difficult and complex to manage. Individual behaviors must be associated with a larger customer organization and interpreted for their impact on the broader customer relationship. Overall, it's fair to say that business-to-business marketers are generally less data- and analytics-oriented than are consumer marketers. So any organization should be capable of adopting the lessons laid out in this book.

Of course, the revolution described here is not finished. More transformational activities in marketing are coming, at SAS and elsewhere. For example, while human marketers will always be present, it's clear that there will be increasing automation in the function. I recently interviewed a member of Adele Sweetwood's marketing staff who is a bellwether of this particular change. His role is to drive certain aspects of digital marketing for SAS, including search engine optimization, digital ad buying, and video ads. Most of the decisions in his role are made by machines using algorithms developed by other machines. He implements and oversees the software for these semi-automated decisions and determines how well it is working. When it needs improvement, he makes adjustments. He is performing tasks that were never performed by humans; there is simply too much data to analyze too quickly for a human to do it. The cognitive technologies he employs are just a straightforward extension of conventional analytics, and SAS is already making some of these cognitive tools available to customers. We will see them increasingly used in marketing and elsewhere at SAS, and perhaps that will be an occasion for another book from Sweetwood. I can't wait to read that one, too.

—Thomas H. Davenport
President's Distinguished Professor of IT and
Management, Babson College
Research Fellow, MIT Initiative on the Digital Economy
Senior Adviser, Deloitte Analytics
Author of *Competing on Analytics* and
Big Data @ Work

THE
ANALYTICAL
MARKETER

INTRODUCTION

Reinventing the Marketing Organization in the Analytical Era

Making the most of analytics, Big Data, and the Internet of Things in the world of marketing is a hot topic, maybe the hottest. Data and analytics are changing how organizations can understand, predict, shape, and continually enhance their customers' experience. But to deliver on that value proposition, marketing needs to undergo a change in culture, talent, structure, roles, responsibilities, and leadership.

While the traditional perception of marketing is very much along the lines of creative types made famous in the TV show *Mad Men*, or even the group that buys pens and T-shirts, the reality is that the best marketers today have a keen sense of and clear focus on the demands of the customer, through sophisticated analytics and data-driven methodologies. In our digital "always on" world, where we're continually collecting copious amounts of real-time data about our customers, marketing is in the best position to own and leverage that data to understand and service the customer in ways that the "mad men" of an earlier era could only dream about. And today's customers—knowing that we have more data about what they buy, use, like, and don't like—are more demanding than ever, expecting us to know and deliver precisely what they want, when they want it. They're also more informed about us; anything they want to know about any company or service provider is right at their fingertips. All of this data—what companies know about customers and what customers know about companies—has forced an evolution in how companies interact with the external world and how they create and sustain relationships with customers. In turn, those changes are driving even bigger internal ones; analytics are driving enormous transformations in how state-of-the-art marketing departments are organized, staffed, led, and run, and even how they interact with other parts of the organization.

In short, everything we have come to consider best practice in how we organize ourselves as a marketing organization will continue to evolve because of the new analytical era we have entered. As powerful as analytics are for transforming your relationships with your customers, they are equally transformative to the marketing organization itself. To fully leverage analytics, marketers have to modernize almost everything they know and do. This has caused a lot of pain and disruption for many of us in marketing and for many marketing organizations.

I know, because I've felt the pain of these changes firsthand. I'm a marketing executive who started out about twenty years ago when marketing was in a totally different era. Now, I run a large marketing organization and have had to navigate many dramatic transformations, not the least of which are the analytics and data, and have had to transform my organization in light of them. I have been on this journey to adjust and adapt my own marketing organization to keep up with the disruption we are all experiencing.

Today, our marketing organization has a new mind-set, a new structure, new talent, and new style of leadership. We needed to shift as an organization from thinking just about the visual and creative components of marketing to embracing a more data-driven and analytical approach to how we shared our messages. That required an evolution in our skill sets and how we went about creating more targeted and intimate conversations with our customers. But in order to accomplish those changes, we needed to rethink how we were organized and how leaders like me went about, well, leading this new kind of analytical marketing organization.

The purpose of this book is to share that experience and to help marketers transform themselves, and their teams, into more analytically driven and more successful professionals in the digital and social era. While there are many books and university courses that cover marketing analytics, data management, and even more on the subject of organizational management, my goal with this book is to provide other marketers like me a unique guide that combines those subjects. In short, this is the book I wish I had had when I led the marketing transformation at SAS. I've written this book to share what we did and how we did it and to provide insights and lessons to others, like you, who are also reinventing your marketing organizations for the digital analytic age. My hope is that in the pages that follow, I provide you with a firsthand, practical account of how to create a new marketing culture that thrives on and adds value through data and analytics. By sharing our story, as well as additional perspectives from other leading companies such as Lenovo, Visa, and Comerica Bank, this book reveals a new set of best practices to help guide your marketing organization's analytical transformation. I am not sure that we always got it right or that we did things in a way that will translate to every organization. We also continue to learn and evolve every day. But my hope is that I can give you the head start I didn't have by sharing our experiences as we went through our metamorphosis.

The Analytically Driven Marketing Organization: A Practical Guide

This book stems from my own experiences as a marketer and as the leader who drove the organizational changes to become an analytically driven marketing organization, but it's fueled by and infused with the inspiration I get from my team. Together we have been on an exciting marketing analytics expedition. Over time, we have identified and established a set of best practices, philosophies, and approaches that have increased our value as a marketing organization by helping us engage with our customers in ways that improve their experiences.

One of the critical lessons I've learned in transforming our marketing organization is to get buy-in and engagement from the key people, "our guiding coalition," on our team. That's why in the pages that follow you'll hear directly from many members of my team who were part of our organization's transformation. Yes, I was helping lead the changes we went through and I share my perspective on that experience. But it was also a highly collaborative effort in which each member of my team played vital roles in our collective transformation. I think you will be inspired by the many voices that continue to drive change across the organization.

Becoming an analytically driven organization isn't only about having the right metrics, methodologies, or technologies in place. In fact, this book will not spend a lot of time discussing analytical tools or methodologies and how to use them. Rather, to drive the kind of change required to meet and shape customer expectations in the age of analytics, fundamental shifts are required in the marketing organization itself: specifically, changes in the marketing mind-set, marketing structure, marketing talent, and marketing leadership.

In this book, I present a practical guide, based on each of those four components, that distills how we've transformed our marketing organization and offers a road map for how others can do the same (see figure I-1):

1. Mind-set—from reactive to proactive

2. Structure—from silos to convergence

3. Talent—from traditional to modern

4. Leadership—from responsive to agile

Each of the four components has its own chapter, and in each chapter, I trace the path of change and offer guidance and advice on how to drive that change in your own organization.

FIGURE I-1

A practical guide for transforming a marketing organization

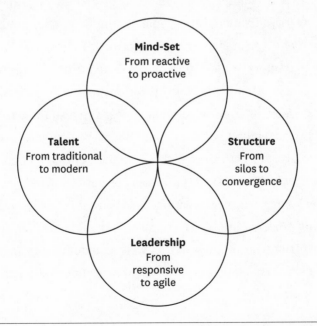

Your Journey Ahead

I've written this book for marketing leadership—marketing managers, marketing executives, and chief marketing officers—as well as for marketing analysts and specialists, campaign managers, digital marketers, and content marketers. If your job involves marketing, then this book is for you. All parts of the marketing organization have to envision, enable, and nurture an analytical culture. I have shared the experiences and evolution that we have gone through as a large, mature organization. Some of the lessons might be different if you run a small organization or even a start-up. I also haven't dug deeply into the specific tools we use to run our marketing organization; you can turn to other books for that help. My hope is that the content here will be relevant from a strategic perspective and supported by practical examples, thoughtful case studies, and best practices to help kick off your own journey to becoming an analytical marketing organization.

Within each chapter, you will read about how SAS and other marketing organizations are implementing analytics, redefining their marketing strategies, and transforming their cultures. Voices include marketers from across the SAS organization in multiple roles and levels, thought leaders on various topics, as well as stories and best practices from select companies. I've also included many sidebars, visuals, and ways to apply my advice to your organization. My favorite features are the "Marketing Analytics at Work" segments, which are stories of transformations from analytical marketers across the organization. There are interviews with chief marketing officers (CMOs), IT executives, thought leaders, and specialists in the field of analytics as well as examples from various industries and companies at different stages of marketing analytics implementation.

The book starts with an introductory chapter outlining why marketing organizations need to change, then follows with a chapter for each component of the four-part guide:

Chapter 1: *Why marketing organizations need to change.* Organizations must evolve from the silo-marketing campaigns of old to the new analytical approach of today. In short, the customer decision journey—how your customers find you—has changed because of the multitude of tools and data now available. Your customers have the ability to control their interactions with you. That means that how you as an organization respond to new customers—while nurturing and retaining existing customers—has also changed.

Chapter 2: *Rethinking your approach.* Marketing has traditionally been a reactive practice: you launch a campaign, wait for the results, and then try again. Now, that's insufficient. In order to connect with the modern customer, you need to embrace a new approach, with data, analytics, and technology that empower you to become proactive, agile, and responsive. This chapter discusses how to employ data and analytics to personalize customer interactions both inbound and outbound, how to nurture customers with the help of analytics, and how to be more agile and proactive than in the past.

Chapter 3: *Realigning structures.* To become an analytical organization, you need to rethink your internal structure. Specifically, you must realign yourself to become customer-centric, by creating a shared path across all channels and developing new partnerships and collaborations across departments inside the organization where marketing teams up with IT, finance, and sales in new ways. That means marketing organizations need to create a converged or unified view of the customer inside the organization, while also forming new interdepartmental relationships with IT, finance, and sales. It also means restructuring how your marketing team members collaborate and learn from each other by adopting best practices such as competency centers to help ensure that skills and knowledge spread through the organization.

Chapter 4: *Hiring the modern marketer.* The days of marketing as simply an artistic endeavor are gone forever. That's not to say that creative skills are not in demand; it's just that they alone are insufficient. Today's modern marketers need a wide variety of skills that include analytics, social media, storytelling, and creativity to be successful. In this chapter are examples of the new jobs we are creating related to analytics and marketing science, new skills and talents we need to hire for, and skills training for existing marketers.

Chapter 5: *Leading the analytical organization.* As an organization evolves to embrace modern marketing principles, it must also promote leaders with the kinds of skills to both orchestrate the talent within and tout the new value of marketing as a powerful source of revenue and insight. We'll discuss topics like how leaders can help cement relationships across the organization and how they can create cross-departmental objectives and reports to drive alignment to customers' needs. It's critical that leaders share the stories of their success as a way to drive home the value of marketing as a bottom-line contributor and not just a cost center.

Conclusion: *Where does an analytical marketer go from here?* The book ends with my thoughts on where we go from here and on how to start your own journey tomorrow. The key to building an analytical marketing organization is, after all, the flexibility to continue to change as the needs of your customer alter over time. That's a challenge we are excited to take on.

Sample Job Descriptions: *What new jobs have we created during our transformation?* The job descriptions I provide in this section would have been invaluable to us several years ago, because they literally didn't exist at the time. We constructed them from scratch. I hope they serve as a shortcut in your transformation.

Organizations like SAS are tapping the power of analytical thinking to drive new connections and conversations with customers by cutting through the increasing noise of the marketplace that threatens to drown out our message. Perhaps, in time, these same lessons can become a part of what business schools teach in the years to come.

We turn first to where it all starts by presenting our case for why the time has come to embrace the future of the modern marketing organization.

1

The Customer Decision Journey Has Changed

The way we market has changed. Gone are the days of one-size-fits-all campaigns, massive e-mail blasts, and measurement of direct mail campaigns by their weight. Relying on a "spray-and-pray" approach simply won't work anymore, because customers expect so much more from us as marketers. Customers now expect their interactions with a brand to have greater immediacy and personalization.

That shift has resulted from the emergence of the broad spectrum of channels that customers now use to interact with us, as well as the fact that customers do not distinguish between offline and online: it's all one company and one experience to them. They want us to know as much about them as possible, provide them the right services, and make them the right offer, regardless of what channels they use to interact with us. It's a theme that crosses all sectors and industries as well.

Let's sum up the landscape we marketers face. The complexity of channels, the volume and complexity of the data, and the sophistication of the customers and their expectations have all shifted. And it's just going to get more complex and more challenging for all of us. We have to get smarter about how we go about our marketing efforts; it's simply not good enough to rely on our gut feelings anymore. We need data to guide our instincts.

Changing customer expectations have forced all marketers to use analytics to understand behavioral trends and better personalize our interactions with customers. "For much of the history of marketing, we didn't really know who was opening the stuff we were sending out," Tom Davenport, the noted analytics expert from Babson College, told me. "But things have changed. We now know how powerful it is to know who is on the other end of our messages and how they are responding to it."

Understanding the Customer Decision Journey

At SAS, we define the term "customer experience" as all of the perceptions and interactions a customer may have with an organization. The experience itself is complicated by a much more convoluted decision or buying journey. By the time customers engage with your company—by visiting your website to download a white paper, for instance—they have traveled through almost 60 percent of their decision journey. That means they have done their homework, networked with their peers, searched through research reports, joined communities, read blog posts, and more. Most of that decision journey now occurs in the digital and social world. This new journey is a complex maze of influences that spans channels and defies consistency. What used to be a very linear relationship has now evolved into something continuous, where people are at various points along the journey. Our customers are now always on, always engaged, and always consuming information.

The challenge we have as marketers is to ensure that we are present and relevant throughout that 60 percent stage (or more) of the customer's decision journey. That challenge continues to grow, as the number of ways in which a customer can connect with your organization in the digital world literally grows daily. Gone are the days when you could simply wait for customers to walk into your storefront to engage with them. Gone, too, is the simplicity of controlling your interactions with your customers through phone calls and snail-mail communications. In the digital and social world we now live in, we can no longer fully control how or where we can make those connections with customers.

Things are going to speed up. Consider the trend in what people are calling the "Internet of Things," a phrase capturing the fact that just about everything in our lives—from our cars and refrigerators to even our toothbrushes—is now linked together and transmitting data about our habits and decisions. By 2020, estimates indicate that 30 billion devices will be connected to the Internet. Can you imagine how much data will result? Are you prepared to take advantage of it?

Customers now have more choices for who to do business with and how—a trend that some have identified as the other hot buzzword, "omni-channel." The challenge for organizations, then, is to be present in whatever channels the customer expects to find them in. In the technology space, customers are more informed and educated than they have ever been. Their peer groups also influence them, and not just when they are looking for solutions.

But rather than relying on what we marketers might call a "peanut butter" strategy of trying to be everywhere equally, we need to be more strategic and deliberate about our outreach. We must understand customer expectations; data and analytics are central to that effort. Marketers now have the data and analytical tools to understand, predict, shape, and enhance the customer experience in ways previously unimaginable. As Jill Dyché, vice president of SAS best practices, framed it for me, "The analytics and post facto understanding of customer information we are generating and collecting is quite possibly the competitive differentiator of the future."

How Do I Get My Organization to Understand the "Why" *Today?*

As a leader, you'll be challenged to get your team members to let go of the traditional methods, investments, and approaches. How can you help them connect the dots? Take the time to figure out what *your* customers look like in the maze of information flow. Analyze the paths that you know they took, ask questions, and tell the story.

1. Define *your* customers' decision or experience journey—the phases that make sense for your product or services. Don't overengineer it. Keep the definition clear and simple.

2. Identify the location of your customers and prospects in their journey based on their actions—what channels, what outcomes, and so on.

3. Leverage the data and analytics to tell your customer's story, and listen to it.

The message is clear: today and into the future, customers or buyers will be coming in and out of cycles at multiple points throughout the journey. The decision-making process is something that remains in constant motion. The job of a marketer is to be *present* and *relevant* in that journey.

For our marketing organization, like so many others, the shift to more digital marketing and channels was certainly the start of being where our customers needed us to be. But we have evolved from simply adding channels to better understanding the value of those channels, as well as the need to align our messages across them (something we'll explore in detail in chapter 3). That also includes rethinking the balance of our outbound marketing efforts—everything we do to get our messages out to customers—with our ability to service and handle inbound requests, or engaging with our customers in their journey. If we do a fabulous job of using digital and social channels to drum up interest in our products, for example, but then fail to welcome that prospect appropriately with, say, an effective landing page that contains information relevant to what that person is searching for, then we haven't completed our work.

This process is also continuous. Consider the example of RCI, part of Wyndham Exchange & Rentals and the Wyndham Worldwide family of brands. The company, which pioneered the concept of vacation exchange in 1974 and altered the way millions of time-share owners experience the world, is no stranger to innovation. That's why, about eight years ago, the organization began its own modernization efforts in how it approached marketing, according to Phil Brojan, senior vice president of global marketing for RCI and other Wyndham Exchange brands. "I still remember the meeting that started it all," Brojan said. "I can remember exactly where people were sitting. We had so many people participating in what we knew was going to be a sea change for RCI that some people had to sit on the countertops of the cabinets around the edge of the boardroom. That was the point at which we all made the commitment that we were going to transform; we were going to become a much more data-driven organization. It was all driven by a simple fact: we were a membership organization that simply didn't know enough about our members. We wanted to make sure we had reliable data to understand our customer better and to make better decisions. And we knew that had to change."

That transformation has enabled the company to segment and model customer data and act on it quickly. "We can personalize communications and sales channels like the web and make them more relevant and timely," Brojan said. Data scientists work within the organization and collaborate with data analysts on advanced analytical techniques like optimization and modeling. "We're seeing more direct attribution of revenue back to campaigns, and we're better able to see what's working and what's not," Brojan added.

The impact of this analytical transformation is enhancing the role of marketing at RCI. Brojan continued, "The insights we glean from the data now help drive overall business strategy. We're providing key indicators of where the revenue opportunities are. This has been huge for marketing at RCI over the past five years, because we're helping set the direction for the company and helping other organizational areas."

Brojan said that analytical marketing organizations like RCI and SAS need to become more predictive in order to anticipate what consumers want before even they know—to recommend and predict more than react. "It's about continuing to personalize the customer experience," he said. "Everyone's come a long way on focusing on the customer experience, yet there is still work to be done. The effort to personalize is never complete."

Rethinking Customer Connection Points

When making their decisions to purchase or repurchase, customers now have much information to work with. They can do their research using different devices and web search tools, or even by tapping into their online and offline social networks. Customers are increasingly relying on comments and ratings to help influence their decisions, which means that, as marketers, you need to stay on top of that information as well. Someone complaining about your products or services can potentially damage your business.

Social channels have a massive influence on the customer's decision journey. But as a marketer, you can't control those channels per se. What you can do is be engaged, present, and relevant in them in a way that builds the trust of your customers and prospects. "Our challenge is to see the customer as a single individual with a rich set of behaviors and preferences," Dyché told me, "while also enabling them to see us via a unified approach and differentiated messaging."

Or, as Jennifer Chase, a senior marketing director at SAS, put it: "For the marketers of the past, the campaign was at the center of everything we did. Now, everything is centered around the customer."

As figure 1-1 shows, we need to employ the power of analytics to understand where a customer is in the decision journey. "If you don't understand where the customer is in their decision journey, you can really be off target with your messaging," said Matthew Fulk, director of marketing sciences and analytics at SAS. With so many channels available to engage with your customers, using e-mail effectively has also never been more important. "A lot has been written about under-standing your customer behavior," Fulk explained. "But understanding where your customer is in their decision journey provides the context you need to move your e-mail marketing from blast to conversation."

Fulk pointed to the unfortunate example of a large business-to-consumer (B2C) retail prospect who had come to us for information about our customer intelligence (CI) software. In fact, two different contacts from the same company were looking at similar information. But, because we hadn't yet realigned our organization for a more uni-fied view of that customer, we ended up sending approximately thirty e-mails (company-wide) combined during a ninety-day period, none of which had anything to do with CI solutions. Rather, we sent informa-tion on Big Data solutions and upcoming user-group meetings for some of our other product offerings. Worse, many of these e-mails came after the prospect had already informed us that he had decided on a competitor's solution instead. Not surprisingly, no one opened or acted on any of the e-mails we sent. They likely ended up in a spam folder.

What we had failed to recognize was that this particular customer was in his "decide" phase, meaning he was ready to choose a vendor to work with. Yet we were treating the customer as if he was still unsure about what he needed. "We could have been sending them

FIGURE 1-1

The SAS customer journey

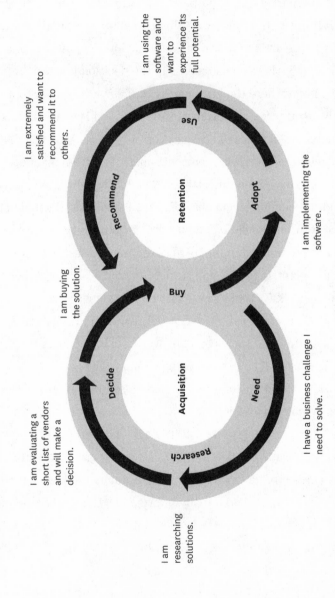

customer success stories and product information tailored to their needs, rather than sending them information on other products they had no use for," Fulk told me.

That example shows why an internal transformation is so necessary. We as an organization can't afford to fall off our customers' radar. Worse, we cannot send the wrong message or strike up a conversation with them on a subject they simply don't have any interest in.

While technology helped us see where the customer was in his journey, we had to also realign our strategy away from product- and solution-based views of the world. In other words, we needed to stop talking about our products and solutions in every channel to every possible person by using much more targeted messaging. But taking that approach also meant that we needed to reorganize so we could govern our engagement strategies and align our channel strategies. The good news is that the tools exist to help tailor messages to the different stages of the decision journey, as long as the organization is structured to best take advantage of them, while also adjusting to the increasing speed of business and the changing needs of customers.

The point is that all this stuff happening in the digital world is affecting the customer's decision journey. We've begun to visualize our customer's decision journey with SAS on the acquisition side and our customer's engagement journey with SAS on the retention side, as shown in figure 1-1. It is an "always on" concept, an infinity loop in which we are all either buying or not buying, with that decision always present as a consideration. Understanding and designing to the phases in your customers' journey, while they are making their way through, will improve their experience with you and positively affect the outcome.

We need to embrace the latest data and tools to ensure we are able to leverage all of the insights and information our customers are providing us along the way. Yes, things are changing fast. But that doesn't change the fact that our customers expect us to change as well, regardless of the industry we are operating in. Even buyers at business-to-business companies are shopping on consumer sites like Amazon and Zappos. That means they see the possibilities and want the same kinds of experiences, whether they are at home or at work.

Analyzing Customer Behavior

As marketers, we need to escape the rigors of list tables and pivot tables. Rather, we need to embrace the data and tools that enable us to see the logical steps a contact followed as she converted into a sales opportunity. By using analytics to examine behavioral data, we can begin to answer such questions as:

1. Did the contact have multiple touch points with marketing before a sale opened or closed?

2. Are there outliers that help us understand how well marketing efforts identified, targeted, and/or nurtured a contact along her journey?

3. Which marketing interactions are most popular in:

    – Helping close a sales opportunity?

    – Creating brand awareness?

    – Generating leads?

4. When analyzing lost sales opportunities, how can we learn which paths ultimately do not benefit our customers or contacts to the point that they lose interest and potentially jump to the competition?

5. Do certain channels relate better for the customer experience and enable quicker movement along the journey?

For SAS, personalization is critical in both the acquisition (demand-generation side of things) and the customer-retention efforts. The level of noise in the technology market space means that we need to be certain our messages and offers align to the behavior of the customer, not just randomly. Behavioral data both online and offline is the differentiator, especially when we can combine it with preference or historical data.

We ask our customers and prospects to give us data about themselves (what they want to tell us) and how they prefer we interact with them. We promise to use it effectively when interacting with them. Sophisticated personalization should replace the concept of special programs (i.e., loyalty cards) that someone has to choose to join. Customers already experience a level of personalization across sites, as when the shoes I just looked at on Zappos happen to show up in an ad on my Facebook page—an example of retargeting.

Marketing Analytics at Work

Moving from Blasts to Conversations

One of the easiest things marketers can do is, when in doubt, send an e-mail blast to get their message out. The approach is predicated on a "strength in numbers" mentality. If you send out enough messages, somebody, somewhere, will receive it and take the desired action.

While blast messages are still used, their value is waning. Why? You are competing for attention with your e-mails, website, advertisements, collateral, events, and any other initiative. People are using their phones, computers, tablets, and TVs to consume information. Now, more than ever, it's harder to reach, much less sway, a customer.

The Challenge

By 2010, SAS marketing efforts included a blend of blasts and more personalized e-mails. The marketing team's goal was to find the right mix of messages and communications methods that would anticipate customers' needs and turn e-mails into a conversation with them on their journey.

The advent of a new customer-journey approach at SAS gave us an opportunity to rethink the e-mail strategy and see what approaches worked best at different phases of the journey. The marketing team looked at historical data on the performance of assets at different phases of the cycle and asked some questions. For example, where along the path is thought leadership more effective than something product specific? And, where is third-party-created content more compelling than content created internally?

The Approach

The marketing team members began assembling data on the customer journey and behavior across each phase. They found examples of customers receiving messages that were out of sync with their actual buying stage.

For instance, a contact would receive messages designed for the early stages of a journey even after the deal was won (or lost). If the contact registered for an asset in one subject area (such as analytics), he would get e-mails about that subject area even if they were associated with a deal for a different solution (such as customer intelligence). Not surprisingly, the contact rarely opened these e-mails.

Marketing analysts also evaluated and identified content gaps across the customer journey. Looking at the totality of interactions, it was clear that building a conversation with the customer would require an overhaul of the e-mail marketing strategy. Here are some key takeaways from the analysis:

- *Scoring* allowed the team to assign a value to all actions, not just registrations. Each interaction with SAS (including web page views, e-mail clicks, and other behaviors) was tracked and added to the score. With more pervasive—and more realistic—scoring of these behaviors, the team could further analyze the relative value of different messages and offers.

- *Segmentation* identified the stage of the customer journey. Once the scoring was complete and applied to contacts, the next phase used the scoring to follow a business rule that identified where the customer was in her journey and what message to send.

- *Automation* provided the foundation for faster, analytics-driven communications. With segments in place, the team created targeted and relevant e-mail communications to provide the right message at the right stage of the customer journey. As the customer progressed through the journey, she got different messages.

- *Analytics* delivered the right business strategy based on the desired outcome. Here, marketing analysts could evaluate how the entire marketing mix was working to move customers through different stages. If customers stalled at a certain point, the analytics could help determine why and trigger an adaptation.

The Results

After this analysis, the team created and refined e-mail campaigns to fit the stages of the customer journey. The content needed for the phases include:

- *Need.* High-level messaging, including industry-specific content and thought leadership strategies (articles, blog posts). Content at this phase explains the problem and provides a path forward.

- *Research.* Content that validates the customer's need to solve the problem. Material here focuses on specific business issues and includes third-party resources (analyst reviews, research reports, etc.).

- *Decide.* Deeper content that provides more product-specific information. This material validates the proposed solution through customer success stories, research reports, product fact sheets, and so on.

- *Adopt.* Onboard and self-service content. This stage focuses on introducing customers to support resources and online communities as well as do-it-yourself material that introduces the customer to the solution.

- *Use.* Adoption content, such as advanced educational information, user conferences, and product-specific webinars. At this stage, users mature with their use of technology and turn to more technical resources to expand their knowledge.

- *Recommend.* Content specific to extending the relationship with the customer. This includes speaking opportunities, focus group participation, and sales references as well as involvement in cross-market and upmarket opportunities.

When customers reach the buy phase, interactions occur primarily between sales and the customer. As a result, customers are typically excluded from e-mail communications.

Eventually, our entire online experience, regardless of site, will be personalized as a way to best engage our customers and prospects and to help ensure we are communicating with them in a way that they prefer. How do we do this? By using customer experience analytics to track, analyze, and then take action when appropriate based on behavior, instead of simply when we want to promote something. In other words, we have adopted an analytical mind-set, which is what we'll discuss in the next chapter.

APPLYING THESE IDEAS TO YOUR ORGANIZATION

How Does Your Organization Interact with Your Customers along Their Decision Journey?

This exercise can reveal how central your customers are to your marketing efforts. You may find, for instance, that your campaigns are the primary focus of your marketing efforts and resources, even though your customers may have shifted their attention elsewhere.

Answer the questions on your own, have your team do the same, and then compare the results. Encourage everyone to be honest and bold; you'll be rewarded as a result.

✓ Do you know where (what channels, offers, etc.) your customers most often interact with your brand?

✓ Are those brand interactions consistent? Do you know when they change?

✓ What data about your prospects, customers, channels, and so on do you collect directly *and* indirectly?

✓ How do you analyze the outcomes—broadly at the summary level, by specific channel or campaign, or others?

✓ Do you monitor and test the relevance of the interactions, such as content performance, lead quality, or A/B testing?

✓ Have you explored new opportunities in the digital marketing world to connect with your customers and prospects?

✓ How well are you able to personalize your messages to your customers during their decision journey? Can you identify where your customers are in the journey, for example, in research or buy phases?

✓ What kind of loyalty and retention strategy does your organization have for existing customers? What is the balance of fixed interactions or programs like newsletters with more organic engagement strategies or social strategies, such as communities?

2

Adopting an Analytical Mind-Set

From Reactive to Proactive

If you want to evolve into an analytical marketing organization, first you need to focus on your mind-set, which is why my guide to change starts here. The evolution of your organization begins by shifting how you and your organization think about using data and analytics in the way you go about marketing.

The shift to adopt an analytical mind-set certainly had an impact on my career. It was initially driven by our need to do a more effective job at measuring the value of what we were doing, especially when considering our impact on the sales pipeline and revenue. And we had to think differently because we now had all kinds of new data and metrics available that would allow us not only to look at effectiveness, but also to identify potential. Measuring impact in a quantitative way was critical. Being able to use analytics in predicting what would work or responding to the customers' behaviors was an even more powerful motivator.

These changes were also forced on us as marketers because, due to the massive influx of new digital channels on the Internet and social media, our customers' expectations had changed. And they continue to change. We understood that if we wanted to respond more effectively to our customers on their decision journey, we needed to build an analytical culture capable of interacting with them in a highly personal and customized manner that was also flexible enough to change directions quickly.

The first step in shifting your organizational mind-set to that of an analytical marketer is changing how you think (and feel) about data.

Be Accountable for Your Data

Everyone on both the consumer and business sides appreciates the value of data—all types and sizes of data, as well as the evolution from Big Data, and the Internet of Things. The key for the analytical marketing organization, regardless of your industry or your customer, is to understand how you can use all that new data to effectively personalize your interactions with your customers. After all, as Emmett Cox, a business intelligence expert who has worked for large organizations like Walmart, GE, and Kmart, writes in his book, *Retail Analytics*, "Data without use is overhead."[1]

Historically, that kind of data expertise lived in a different part of the organization, most likely in IT. If you wanted data in the form of a report or some such, you would submit a request to IT and wait until you got what you asked for. That's no longer viable. Analytical marketers are now producers as well as consumers of data, which is changing how we have to structure partnerships within our organization (something we will dig into in the next chapter) and the kind of people and skill sets we hire (a subject we'll explore in more detail in chapter 4).

Data is the holy grail of marketing analytics, whether big or little, complex or simple, structured or unstructured. That's because all data tells a story. The most valuable data, as well as the most complex, is customer data. Once you have good, clean data to work with, you can then begin to apply analytical tools so you can make proactive decisions based on the stories that the data is telling you about your customers and prospects. If you begin to see data as the "author" that is sharing trends, helping you identify behaviors, and measuring the value of your activity along the journey, you will truly appreciate the impact it can have on all elements of marketing.

The key is that you and your whole marketing organization need to shift your mind-set so that you understand the importance of data. It's your responsibility to collect it, care for it, and establish rules for governing your data. Cox told me that, while most organizations have moved to embrace their data, they've also fallen prey at times to collecting data for data's sake, without first taking in the business value of that data. "Too often, organizations start chasing the next shiny object like social media before they've optimized everything they already have," he said. A good rule of thumb in making sure you are collecting the right data is to ask yourself what three things about your business are keeping you up at night. If you are collecting data that will help address those concerns, then you're on the right path.

So what are some other components of a sound data strategy?

- Volume

- Source

- Complexity

- Structure

- Quality

- Relevance

- Integration

Our experience with a data strategy is that it is a continuous process. Even with all the tools at our disposal, data collection, management, and governance are challenging. As you grow and change, your needs will continue to shift direction. The way we sell, market, and support our customers has morphed through the years, affecting the type and volume of data we have. For marketing, we've continued to expand our data sources in an effort to gather more and more information on our customers, especially from preference and behavioral perspectives.

Our journey as an organization to better embrace the stories behind the data we were collecting began in 2009 when we modernized our approach. Until that time, we had relied on a disparate array of data sources, mostly dozens of spreadsheets, to track our marketing campaigns and responses. It was largely managed manually and on an ad hoc basis, which created huge hurdles every time we needed to create a contact list for a new campaign. Sometimes it took up to three months just to build an accurate list we could use as part of a promotion. In time, we began to realize how untenable that kind of system was.

That's why we shifted direction and began to implement what we call our data mart, which is quite simply a structured source that pulls together all the disparate data that used to live in spreadsheets. With our data all in one place and updated daily, we could begin to paint a full picture of our customers, because we could, for the first time, see how all of their different behaviors were connected. For example, in the past, we might have lost track of which contacts at which customers we had reached out to during certain campaigns, and how they responded. "A lot of marketers have access to web analytics and behavioral data," Matthew Fulk, a marketing director at SAS, said. "The differentiator is learning to ask the right questions about the data and making it a priority to do so."

A powerful aspect of the data we were now collecting was what people were doing on our website, something we call "customer experience analytics," or CXA. We now knew how much time customers were spending on our website, what they were looking at, which white papers they downloaded, what videos or webinars they watched, and so on. That all combined with more transactional records, such as installation records on a customer's software service record or how many times a customer called tech support and why, as well as offline behaviors, such as when a customer attended a conference or event and what he or she did there.

Through our data mart, we also began to tie customer behaviors back to building sales pipelines and generating revenue. In other words, the data we now captured could tell us that $X of the pipeline eventually turned into revenue and could be tied to which outbound or inbound marketing actions we took.

Added up, that meant we now had a much more complete picture of our customers based on the breadth of the data we could collect, store, and, perhaps most importantly, analyze. We had new opportunities to apply our analytical tools to examine customers' different behaviors, depending on where they happened to be in their decision journey.

Data needs to be clean and accurate; otherwise, your analysis and, ultimately, your decisions could be flawed. Now and then, you'll need to rebalance it. Look for sources you no longer need or data that isn't providing value and get rid of it. Reinvest your resources where you're getting returns. Help the data tell the story so the analytics can learn from it. In our marketing organization,

Creating a Data Mart

A common challenge in customer data is consistency, especially with the increase in unstructured data from text sources in mobile and social channels. When we began collecting and governing our marketing data so we could gain insights into our customers' decision journeys, we created a platform, or data mart, that helped us standardize and create connections between various sources that enabled us to paint dynamic pictures of what our customers wanted.

A Hundred Data Elements from Four Key Sources

- Sales database

  - Leads

  - Pipeline

  - Invoices

- Marketing database

  - Online and offline interactions

- Customer database

  - Training

  - Publications

we focused an initiative on data source performance and were able to eliminate the poorest-performing investments. The data gave us the confidence to let go, which translates to cost savings and increased effectiveness.

- User groups

- Installation

- Tech support

• Purchased data

Some additional examples of the kind of data that we track to better understand customers' decision journeys and their progress are:

• Live event attendance

• Website traffic

• Technical support queries

• Customer satisfaction survey data

• Customer reference activity

• Webinar attendance

• White paper downloads

Having a reliable and clean source of data to work with is critical. Those using reports or analysis can lose confidence when something doesn't seem correct in the outcome. The first place they blame is the data, and when they lose confidence in the data, all sorts of problems result. When everyone in the entire organization takes full accountability for the value of the data and its care and feeding, and they truly know the data, the results are strong. The confidence level in decision making is high, the level of innovation is robust, and the impact is evident.

The Data Oath

Your analytics will only be as good as your data. The marketing organization's job is to develop a culture of respect, care, and maintenance of data.

1. Protect the data

    - Establish and enforce the governance.

    - Define a clear process and joint accountability.

    - Leverage expert methodologies and technology.

2. Respect the data

    - Make data quality everyone's job—both internally and externally (don't let bad data sources into your data).

    - Ask questions about the data; get to know it well.

    - Have only one version of the truth; kill the spreadsheets.

3. Love the data

    - Don't blame the data (or each other).

    - Listen to the story the data is telling.

    - Provide unconditional support for and nurture your data.

When you are open to hearing the stories it can tell you, data will likely lead you to a particular point of view. Done right, data digging will bring you to conclusions and additional questions. This provides the foundation upon which you can make solid business decisions. Unfortunately, all too often, we can fall into the trap of using data to confirm a presupposition or bias. That's why the data by itself isn't enough.

From Mad Men to Math Men and Women

This is no longer the era of Don Draper, the now infamous lead character in the TV show *Mad Men*. The series, set in New York City during the 1960s and 1970s, followed the exploits of an ad agency and its various clients. Draper was like a magician, a creative genius who always seemed to know what kind of campaign the clients would fawn over. But we're in the middle of a shift where data and analytics, not the creative talent in the art department, drive the success of a marketing campaign.

Marketing has traditionally been considered an "art"—a practice based on creativity, gut-based decision making, and no real expectations that it could directly affect the firm's bottom line. But the shift in the science means that marketing has come into its own and evolved to what we're calling "marketing analytics." Marketing now is more about science or math that is driven by an influx of data, channels, mobility, and, most importantly, changing customer demands.

Rather than relying on Don Draper types, we're leaning more on the work of folks who help analyze behavioral data and the digital footprint of our customers and prospects. They produce reports that lead to campaigns more focused on where customers are in their decision journey and what they are looking for.

The term *forensics* has entered everyday marketing vernacular. Typically associated with the use of science and technology to establish facts in a criminal case, data forensics refers to the practice of using data discovery to establish the facts of a marketing activity, campaign, or broader initiative. But beyond the basics of data digging, data forensics incorporates intangibles—the piecing together of anecdotal and qualitative tidbits along with quantitative data to develop a rich picture of performance. The combination of qualitative and quantitative data provides the context necessary for sound decision making.

Marketing Analytics at Work

Finding Your Customers' BFFs

One of the most powerful sales tools is often something that you can't foresee or control. Even though customers read papers, visit websites, and talk with a salesperson, another factor can make all the difference: a referral from a friend or coworker.

Consider the way that sites like Google, Yelp, and others have changed the way consumers make everyday decisions, such as choosing restaurants. You can go to the restaurant nearest you or one you've visited before. Or, you can try something new by looking at your smartphone to see which dining spot has the highest ratings or the best reviews. Why? People place a premium on the personal experience of those in their networks.

For business-to-business software companies like SAS, the impact of customer advocacy is critical. These influencers can set the tone and provide a consistent positive influence throughout the customer journey. Unfortunately, this type of advocacy is tough to measure and hard to predict.

The Challenge

Although a customer may be a single record in your database, she doesn't exist in a vacuum. Each contact has a connection to others within her business or the industry. Understanding and fostering good relationships can have a huge effect on your retention and loyalty efforts.

During the effort to formalize a new customer journey, the SAS marketing team began to focus on different phases of this cycle. The customer journey contained the following phases:

- Acquisition, which includes need, research, decide, and buy

- Retention, which includes adopt, use, and recommend

On the retention side, the team knew from anecdotal evidence that some SAS customers were advocates of the technology and for the company overall. In fact, several SAS geographies and divisions had data confirming the idea that finding and rewarding high-value customers led to big returns. What was lacking was an overarching program for getting customers to advocate for SAS technology.

For a larger effort, the team assessed the customer behavior data, examining those who attended events, provided feedback on surveys, sent ideas to R&D, and generally stayed engaged with the company. From a revenue standpoint, those people were often the ones advocating for the use of new SAS technologies or the expansion of existing deployments.

What was less understood was the reach of these influencers and how their activities affected others within the account. With that information, SAS could identify more advocates and nurture that behavior.

The Approach

The SAS marketing team members started by digging into the data that they had on customers. They first identified a segment of the top accounts, which contained more than twenty thousand individual contacts. Once identified, the team began to examine the behaviors exhibited by that group:

- Live event attendance

- Website traffic

- Technical support queries

- Customer satisfaction survey data

- Customer reference activity

- Webinar attendance

- White paper downloads

This information provided a better understanding of the range of activities that customers undertake. However, simply cataloging the behaviors wasn't enough. The team applied a scoring model for different types of interactions. This allowed the team to weight certain activities, helping further identify which customers were the best advocates—"BFFs," or "best friends forever," as the marketing team began to call them.

The Results

SAS marketing used the information to create a model that is the foundation for customer-focused data exploration. The initial effort helped shed light on how influential advocates can shape retention and additional sales. As a result, sales and marketing worked together to highlight BFFs within key accounts in an ongoing effort to foster better relationships with those key individuals.

Initiatives to locate and encourage advocates used the model to identify the likely candidates within customer organizations. The team then designed campaigns and outreach efforts to give these advocates the tools to foster and expand their influence.

The marketing team now focuses on advocacy campaigns that target potential BFFs. The goal is to build more SAS advocacy during the recommend phase of the customer journey (see figure 2-1).

Title: Customer "Best Friend" Analysis

FIGURE 2-1

Customer "best friend" screenshot

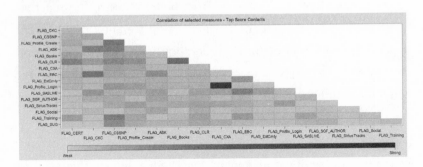

What: Scores and analyzes customer behaviors and determines which behaviors are most highly correlated.

Value: Groups customers into high-, medium-, and low-engagement categories and identifies behavior trends that are most commonly grouped together.

- The goal is to keep your customer as a best friend and identify opportunities to create more best friends.

- Identifies cross-promotion opportunities.

- Identifies opportunities to better service the customer.

When you add analytics and visualization tools to your marketing toolbox, you can begin to tell stories from the data that you have worked so hard to cultivate and harness. Essentially, you have created "the art of analytics" or the art of analytical storytelling—the perfect blend of art, science, marketing, and math. You can begin to see connections you had missed otherwise. You can also see how the story changes when you make changes. You can then begin asking what-if questions to see what kinds of new stories you can begin to tell. That's how you can shift from being reactive to proactive, to create the future rather than just being weighed down by the past. The better you begin to understand how to tell the stories, the more you become empowered to ask additional questions and to see if you can find even more data to expand on the themes you've uncovered.

We've also seen this lesson in companies we work with. Take, for example, the credit card company Visa. In a company that size, it's obvious that there's a sophisticated marketing machine behind its portfolio of digital advertising, television commercials, sporting event sponsorships, and credit card offers. Maintaining a position of leadership in the financial space requires complex processes, critical and creative thinking, and, according to analytics executive Ramkumar Ravichandran, a pervasive, analytical mind-set.

As director of analytics and A/B testing at Visa, Ravichandran supports executives, leaders, and decision makers in product, marketing, sales, and relationships. He explained to me that "we are the custodians of the data, so our responsibility is to enable our users to have confidence in the decisions they make using that data."

One of the biggest changes the analytical era of marketing has brought about is that things need to happen much faster than before. "We used to have a very linear approach," Ravichandran told me. "Now when something is going live, there's already an immediate need to respond. We need to be able to take action on the fly." Because of those changes, marketers can no longer think about analytics as something that supports them or a function that just one person, like a chief digital officer, would perform. Rather, analytics is now an integral part of marketing's value chain.

Ravichandran said that numbers by themselves are historical. That's why, while data is needed to inform campaigns, at the end of the day, it still comes down to marketers using their gut feelings to make the best decision possible. "And we can use data and analysis to inform and guide us in the right direction," he added.

Because data and analytics are now so intertwined with marketing strategy, expectations for leadership on the marketing side have changed. "It's no longer acceptable to say you're a marketer, but you're not a numbers person," Ravichandran said. "Executives are demanding more data literacy as a precursor for being a good marketer." And it's not just in the marketing space. He added, "All of our chief executives are comfortable with numbers and data-driven approaches."

Ravichandran was quick to clarify, however, that a focus on data, numbers, and quantified measures should not replace the value of vision: "I have an enormous respect for data, but I also believe all of it has to be driven by strategy, the business case, benchmarking against the industry, all those things that provide a broader perspective. You have to understand what specific metrics you're trying to impact with your actions." He advocates the importance of understanding your company's business model, applying and measuring the right metrics, and truly understanding your competitive position and your customers' needs.

The big mind-set shift we need to make, therefore, is recognizing how our intuition is now informed by data and analytics. When someone comes to a marketing manager or leader with a proposal to spend, say, $250,000 on a campaign, she had better come armed with data, analysis, testing plans, and expected outcomes, as well as what her gut is telling her.

Of course, marketers have always relied on a variety of metrics for measuring their campaigns. One prominent example is the response rate to a specific campaign. Those kinds of metrics give us something to react to. Metrics tell us where we have been, where we are now, and how we performed compared to a previous year. They paint both a historical perspective and a current status, but they fall short in revealing what's next. The new reality is that reacting to metrics isn't enough. Customers now have greater expectations about what they expect us, as marketers, to know and how we interact with them.

By contrast, a sustainable marketing analytics strategy needs to be equipped with advanced analytics, so we can begin answering questions such as:

- Where is the opportunity?

- Where should I invest next? Or differently?

- What needs to change?

- What is the full story that my data is telling me?

- How do I stay ahead of the customer's expectations?

Today's analytical marketers need the kind of data they can use to become proactive, predictive, and agile enough to make changes quickly and easily. We need to employ better tools that allow us to talk to our customers and prospects based on their location in the decision journey. We need to interact differently with our customers, to better personalize how we respond, when and how they find us. Advanced analytical capability and approaches enable marketers to make fact-based decisions about design, audience segmentation, channel optimization, inbound marketing, and nurturing efforts. Unlike in the past, marketers are now able to deliver valuable information about trends and the digital dialogue of customers and prospects.

For example, if a sales lead comes from a live event we host, we need to have more information on that prospect's behavior, such as:

- After the conference, what web pages did he view?

- How long was each visit to the website?

- What assets did he download?

- What other activities did he participate in—webcasts, other conferences, sales calls?

With this data, you can start to assemble a picture of how every part of the marketing spectrum affects a sale (see figure 2-2). The figure shows a snapshot of a contact at an individual company, but we could look at similar metrics for everyone in the company and beyond. The value of information expands exponentially when you start to evaluate the aggregate behaviors of hundreds, thousands,

FIGURE 2-2

Digital footprint screenshot

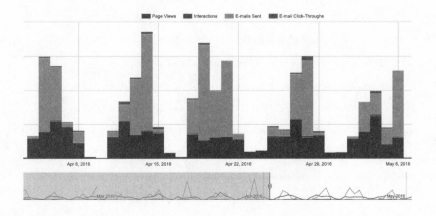

or millions of contacts. With this level of data, you can build a better picture of customers' behavior and start to assemble marketing programs designed to anticipate their demands.

But it's essential to note that the element of art in marketing isn't going away. The opposite is true. "Data is definitely not the answer 100 percent of the time," Shawn Skillman, a senior marketing data visualization analyst at SAS, explained. "It's just a mind-set shift where we can use the numbers to help us make better decisions than when we relied simply on our gut." Science or analytics has actually enhanced the art elements of a campaign by empowering marketers with fact-based decision making and insight beyond what they ever imagined.

Another important aspect to this shift is that the more we rely on the facts that analytics helps us uncover, the less biased we become about the kinds of campaigns we run as well as who we target with them. In other words, we don't want our gut to cause us to go places we could have avoided if we had first looked to the data for clues about what might work well and what wouldn't. "We have become outcome agnostic," said Scott Sellers, a segmentation analyst at SAS who exemplifies the kind of analytical marketer we are grooming. "From an analytical standpoint, we don't have a dog in the fight. Our job is to show someone how we got the data and how we interpreted it. My whole goal is to give logical reasons why we reached a certain conclusion. You may reach a different conclusion based on your interpretation, so let's have a conversation about that."

Marketing has shifted from functioning purely as an outbound effort into one more receptive to a high volume of inbound opportunities. Customers and prospects are 60 percent of the way through their decision-making journey as they learn about our products and solutions through visiting websites, downloading content, joining communities, and chatting online, among other things.

Now we have a two-way interaction with customers as they proceed on their decision journey; there is much more emphasis on inbound marketing efforts than the outbound activities of the past. But inbound marketing demands a whole new set of analytics that help us understand the experience and behavior of the customer. "It's not about building lists anymore," Fulk told me. "It's about putting the customer's behavior at the forefront and thinking strategically from there." It's also about learning to leverage both inbound and outbound efforts to maximize our chances of connecting with our customers in a way that they're most interested in. We still need to get out our outbound messages, but by fine-tuning where we target the audience, we can then stimulate additional inbound opportunities because we've sparked someone's interest. If we write a post for a popular blog on, say, customer intelligence, that might then spur a potential customer to visit our site later on to learn more about our offering on the way to becoming a solid sales lead. "Your outbound and inbound efforts have to be symbiotic," Jennifer Chase, a senior marketing director at SAS, said. "You won't have any visitors to your website, for example, unless you are doing the necessary outbound activities to drive them there." And, then we have to have the relevant inbound strategies to follow up.

When you combine outbound marketing data with inbound marketing data, and then apply advanced analytics, for instance, you begin to shift to a more proactive marketing strategy that measures value. Marketers are then enabled beyond gut instinct toward fact-based decisions. They are not simply making static recommendations, but instead personalizing offers based on behavior and demographics. We no longer have to make assumptions about what customers are doing, because we have the data pieces to better understand where they are in their decision journey and what they might want to talk to us about.

In the big-picture context, marketing has shifted from a function that involved saying what you wanted to say into a mechanism that communicates what the customer actually wants to hear. Put another way, by using marketing analytics, we no longer have to rely on just telling

Marketing Analytics at Work

How Analytics Empower Campaign Agility

A common practice in traditional marketing is to first choose a target market to focus on. You then align your organization's strategies and messaging to create a campaign in that target market. But what happens when it becomes clear that the campaign you created isn't working? How agile are you in terms of adjusting on the fly and adapting to the needs of your prospective customers?

The Challenge

A campaign we ran at SAS was targeted at small to medium-sized businesses, or SMBs. We felt we needed to come up with some tailor-made messaging for this group, which would be distinct from similar campaigns we were launching targeted at larger, enterprise-level companies. To do that, we highlighted what we thought were business needs, language, and case studies that would resonate most with the SMBs.

But after the program launched and began running, the results were disappointing: we saw lower than expected results for performance metrics, including click-through rates, conversions, and conversion rate. So we tweaked the messaging, offers, and program structure in ways we thought might improve results. After crunching the numbers again, the results came in: the campaign was still floundering.

We were now forced to take a fresh look at the situation. What had we done wrong? After some reflection, we also came upon an even more telling question: Did we actually need to separate the SMBs from the larger organizations? We had begun with an underlying assumption that we needed to treat the SMB market differently. Had that been a mistake?

The Approach

To help guide us forward, we selected a roster of key performance metrics to analyze:

- E-mails sent

- Open rate

- Click-through rate

- Opt-out rate

- Conversions (those who filled out registration forms to receive the promoted asset)

- Conversion rate

- Lead-generated SSOs (internal metric that measures the number of conversions we score as leads who progress to become a sales opportunity)

- Rate of completed leads to lead-generated SSOs (internal metric that measures the percentage of conversions scored as leads who progress to become a sales opportunity)

We then looked at how the SMBs responded to the SMB-specific campaign compared to how they responded when they received the enterprise-level messaging.

The Results

Much to our surprise, the SMB targets responded more strongly to the enterprise-level campaign (see table 2-1). Our assumption had been proved wrong. So we adjusted by closing down the

TABLE 2-1

SMB lead nurture responders

Metric	Non-SMB programs	SMB programs
Sent	26,881	37,025
CTR	9.50%	2.50%
Open rate	22.16%	12.71%
Opt-out rate	0.40%	0.50%
Registered	1,410	328
Conversion rate	5.29%	0.90%
Lead-generated SSOs	18	3
Completed lead to lead-generated SSO rate	5.40%	3.50%

SMB-specific campaign and then retargeted the SMBs with our enterprise-level messaging instead.

The key takeaway for us was a reminder that we cannot afford to let our own assumptions about the market hinder our ability to adjust to the needs of our customers. In this situation, we relied on the power of analytics to provide the answers about what people wanted rather than continue on in a losing cause.

everybody about everything we are doing. "It used to be that marketers would spend their time and energy promoting their own products and events to whomever would listen," Julie Chalk, a marketing manager at SAS, told me. "We have now flipped this model. Using analytics we now start by analyzing the audience and seeing what the data tells us. That way, we can understand who we are trying to go after. Instead of just pushing out the message we might want to say, we can now meet people at whatever stage they are in their decision journey."

We can meet customers along their decision journey by relying on advanced analytics, which can increase the quality of a marketing campaign by using tools like scoring, optimization, and predictive capabilities. The standard spreadsheet-based reports that marketers used to rely on to see how their campaign performed have now shifted to interactive visualization dashboards they can use daily to track the efficacy of their campaign, while making changes on the fly when necessary to ensure a campaign is making the most of its potential. The biggest difference is that marketers now have these tools at their disposal; we no longer have to submit requests to the IT department to get this information (we will dig into the partnership between marketing and IT in chapter 3).

Embrace Marketing Agility

With analytical tools, we can now better target and personalize our outreach to customers as well. We no longer have to put ads for our products everywhere. Rather, we can target people who likely want to see ads for our products, which results in more effective campaigns and investments, and a better experience for the customer.

Consider an example in which we ran a campaign for one of our software products. In the past, when we might have run a direct mail campaign, someone like Julie Chalk did analysis on the back end to determine who responded to the campaign and who didn't. Meanwhile, the campaign team simply moved on to its next project, and everyone learned from the experience. But that's all changed. Now with digital campaigns, Chalk is able to monitor the effectiveness of a campaign in real time. If we're trying to encourage prospects to sign up for a webinar, for example, Chalk can analyze the kinds of behavior those prospects are exhibiting when they show up at our website. She might see that some 26 percent of people who land on the sign-up page decline to register for the webinar, which then gives her license to ask why that happened and what adjustments we need to make to increase that conversion rate. "I love this transition from just looking at reports the next day to being able to keep trying and adjusting," Chalk told me. "We have so much data now available at our fingertips. And it's fun to experiment with ways we can use it to make the best decisions possible." Customers are always on, and so are we.

As another example, it's great to know that a prospect who attended a live event converted to a sales lead and, ultimately, a sales opportunity, which is our phrase akin to a "sales pipeline." What is more insightful, however, is learning to understand the behavior that specific contact exhibited before and after the marketing live event. This is the practice of what we call "pathing analysis," meaning "what path did a customer take to turn into a sale?"

By looking at figure 2-3, which illustrates the activity a prospect took on her way to becoming a customer, which we call "the happy path," we can answer such questions as: Did this particular contact download a white paper to do her research before investing her time

FIGURE 2-3

Pathing analysis screenshot

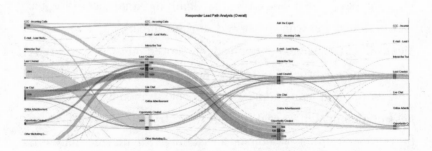

and energy into attending a vendor-sponsored live event? What happened following the live event? Was the sales organization the only team that engaged with the contact? Did the contact register for or attend additional marketing events to further and fully vet the product she was interested in purchasing? If so, what was the logical trail of marketing events that made this contact comfortable enough to agree to become a sales lead and ultimately a sales opportunity? Skillman explained that "with pathing analytics, we are able to peer into the behaviors of our current and prospective customer base. Displaying a flow of data from one website or event to the next can enable us to capture and gauge interest in a product or solution. The value is to model behavior for opportunities, such as a win, loss, or sales pipeline, and superimpose that profile on top of our current customers to influence the desired outcome. We can reduce churn and better enhance content marketing and make the customer journey more efficient."

By using tools and analytical approaches like pathing analysis, we can get answers to such questions as:

- Which marketing interactions are most useful in helping close a sales opportunity? In creating brand awareness? In generating useful leads?

- Did the contact have multiple touch points with marketing before a sale opened or closed?

- What behaviors are outliers but still useful for understanding how well marketing efforts identified, targeted, and/or nurtured a contact along his journey?

What becomes complicated, though, is that we can't get trapped into giving too much credit to any one action we have taken, something we marketers call "attribution." In the past, whatever led to the last click or contact got all the credit for a customer conversion. But in a multichannel world, it's no longer that simple. Every company struggles with attribution, because assigning credit or allocating marketing dollars to activities that seem to be working more than others can get tricky. But it's difficult to assign credit or give attribution to any one activity. It's often a mix of the many things you are doing, both outbound and inbound, that works in combination to turn a prospect into a customer. The answer, then, is that we need to keep pushing with our understanding of the paths customers use, and then use our analytical capabilities to change, along with how the customer is changing. "Attribution must take into consideration the cost for the marketer as well as the cost for the customer," Skillman said. "Cost being not only hard costs, but also soft costs, such as time to travel and time spent engaged with a website, webinar, live event, and so on. Each company will have specific needs to complete a true attribution puzzle. One may start with a first-touch model or a model that gives 'credit' to each touch point to start. This will paint a very rudimentary picture from which each business can tweak and add in more complex business requirements."

We relied previously on static information to launch a marketing campaign. Say, for example, we knew that a potential customer once downloaded a white paper on a piece of technology we offer. We used the information we gathered on that customer to keep her updated on that same technology. But what if that customer's needs and interests changed? What if, by sending along the same information, we were now annoying that potential customer? On the other hand, if we use our dynamic data and analytical tools to find out what that potential customer is currently interested in looking at, we can then adjust the kind of information we are sending her in a campaign that's relevant to her current interests.

Again, this is a big switch from how we used to launch campaigns, a practice you might call mass marketing. We had a database-marketing analyst create a list of people to market to solely based on guidelines the campaign manager provided. The analyst would then build the list using those criteria, which might involve variables like someone's title, industry, or purchase history. When the list was complete, the campaign manager would then implement the campaign. But what if the criteria were outdated? How effective would that campaign be?

Today, we can use our latest data to track everything from how often someone has been on our site, what support tracks he might have open, which classes he has attended, what campaigns we have already marketed to him, and more, all of which help build his dynamic profile. Even if the list of names we build for a campaign is smaller than in the past, the results far exceed what we once got.

Making this shift can actually be difficult for some marketers who still struggle with the notion that their list isn't big enough. But that reaction is based on the kind of response rate they have become accustomed to. Let's say you wanted to get fifty people to respond to a particular campaign. How many names would you need to get that kind of response: ten thousand, fifty thousand, or a hundred thousand? Who knew? But today, using data and analytical tools like scoring, segmentation, and modeling, you might be able to get a near 100 percent response rate to a campaign.

Another example involves traditional print advertising. Running a single ad in a national magazine might cost $30,000 to $50,000. Not only is that extremely expensive, it is also difficult if not impossible to measure the effectiveness of those ads. Yes, there are ways to try and capture how someone reacts to an ad, like including a URL on it or a special phone number to call. But how many people actually respond to those things?

When you launch a similar digital campaign, you not only can reach a broader audience, but also can literally track how people respond to it. I admit that it took me some time to adjust to the possibilities this new approach offered. But the more I saw the effectiveness of analytics, the more we began to push them throughout our organization. And the better we got at embracing analytics, the better stories we were then able to tell to our leadership team, which helped us build internal support for getting to the next level of analytical techniques.

In building an analytical culture in marketing, you are essentially creating the foundation for operationalizing all of the different types of analytics that you will need to inform, evaluate, and drive decisions. If you want to operationalize all of the various forms of analytics for the various audiences, then you must put those analytics to use. For our organization, we exercised our analytical muscle across the entire global department; analytics are on every desktop and are part of every conversation. You don't need a single analytics approach; you need several that build off each other and continually challenge your organization.

Some of the most powerful uses of analytics involve marketing optimization techniques through which we can dramatically decrease opt-out rates and increase conversion rates. Optimization and modeling are pivotal in campaign design, list segmentation, and, ultimately, campaign execution. Scoring and web analysis anchor inbound nurturing campaigns, allowing us to better engage website visitors who arrive via search marketing and other sources. If marketing can see the digital dialogue and footprint a prospect has brought along with her on her journey, the opportunities are endless.

Scoring, for instance, helps us better discern how well a lead will convert to a sales opportunity. In the past, we considered anyone who performed a predefined action on the site a lead and passed that lead along to sales. While seeming like a good idea at the time, it was really more of a volume game than one based on precision. As a result, sales had to sift through these leads to find the best ones. Now, by using our data and analytical tools, we can do a lot of that prescreening before we ever send any lead to sales.

We have developed different sets of rules to help us answer the question of how good a lead someone might be, such as evaluating the prospect's job function, the size of his company, and his title when he registered, for example, to download a white paper. Based on the rules we have established, we can then assign a prospect a score that tells us the most appropriate actions we should undertake with him.

As you can see in figure 2-4, if a prospect scores highly on both her implicit actions and on her profile, we consider her ready to hand over to our sales team. If the prospect scores well on only one of the two valuations, then we move her into what we call a "nurture" program, which essentially means that we will follow up with some relevant e-mails and messaging to learn more about how she might evolve into a stronger sales prospect. If someone scores low on both counts, we'll then put that contact on a "watch" list, where we might set an automatic reminder to follow up with her in three months as a way to reevaluate her interest. We have also employed more sophisticated scoring models that align to the performance of certain channels and preferences.

FIGURE 2-4

Customer scoring dimensions

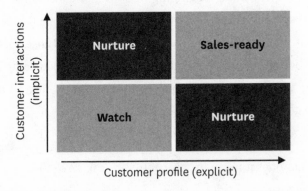

Events and users groups are another area within our scope of marketing offerings that have been completely transformed by analytics. Before we dove deeply into the world of analytics, many of our marketing efforts involved hosting events as a way to drum up interest in our products and solutions. They seemed to work well: it was a great opportunity to connect with prospects and customers face-to-face and find out exactly what they might be interested in. Event marketing remains a critical channel for reaching customers and prospects; nothing can replace human interaction.

But events also have a downside. They cost a lot to organize in terms of both time and money. And while we could collect metrics on which attendees eventually bought a product, calculating the return on investment (ROI) from a live event wasn't always clear. To be sure, there were less tangible brand-building benefits we could collect from hosting events. But we began to ask ourselves if that was good enough anymore, now that we had seen the potential of our digital campaigns. "We began to wonder what we could accomplish if we shifted resources from events to more paid search," Chase told me. "Instead of reaching a few hundred people at a time, we could be reaching thousands instead. It became a question of scale and how could we speak to more of the market."

As an example, our field marketing team had been implementing nationwide road shows beginning in 2013 and continuing into 2015 to raise awareness and generate leads for one of our flagship products. But in May 2015, we analyzed how effective those road shows were to better understand the impact of this extended campaign and whether we could spend resources in more efficient and effective ways to generate interest in the product.

As a way to measure that, we asked questions about the data such as:

- What does it mean in this context to ask, "Are the road shows effective?"

- What were the registration and attendance numbers?

- What were the no-show percentages?

- How many leads were generated?

- How many sales opportunities (SSOs) were generated from those leads?

- Did the contacts come to the events with a preexisting SSO or did those deals open as a result of the event?

- Do certain road show locales perform better than others?

- What was the return on investment?

Once we knew what questions to ask, we ran the numbers in several ways to account for one big deal that had skewed the numbers. We ultimately found that:

- Only one road show was associated with multiple wins (two), so there were no obvious geographies where we should focus our attention.

- Only two associated wins contained related products.

The end result of that analysis—which showed a relatively low ROI from road show–style events—led our organization to make a somewhat radical shift in the number of events we host each year, cutting that figure from 190 to 80, a decision that made some members of our sales team somewhat uneasy. Fortunately, as an analytical marketing organization, we have developed a sense of trust and partnership with sales, a dynamic we will discuss in more detail in chapter 3.

Embracing analytical marketing tools and techniques not only gives you better results, but also allows you to become more flexible and responsive. The ability to make decisions more quickly, alter investment strategies, change channels, adjust volumes, and test new approaches means that as an organization, you will be more relevant. By making the mind-set shift to embrace analytical thinking, you also gain the ability to make adjustments on the fly; you don't need to wait six months to see whether your campaign was effective or not. The data and analysis will tell you in real time what's happening, which gives you the opportunity to make changes and tweaks, also in real time, based on how customers are responding. That's powerful and empowering across the organization.

APPLYING THESE IDEAS TO YOUR ORGANIZATION

Is Your Marketing Organization Agile Enough to Support an Analytical Mind-Set?

You and your team should answer the following questions to see where your marketing organization is currently positioned along the analytical spectrum. Use this opportunity to assess how you treat your data, what tools you're employing to leverage insights from that data, and then assess how nimble you are to take advantage of those insights. While there are no right answers here, your responses will shed some light on gaps and opportunities for your organization to pursue.

- ✓ How long does it take to design, test, and execute a digital campaign?

- ✓ How many people and how many different systems are involved in delivering marketing campaigns?

- ✓ How quickly can you respond to a market-based hot topic?

- ✓ How quickly can you respond to a customer interaction or request?

- ✓ How long do you take to adopt a new channel? Do you have any focus on emerging channels and a testing plan?

✓ How long do you wait to find out results?

✓ Do your marketers have access to all of the data and analytics they need to make changes to their campaigns?

✓ How risk averse is your organization?

✓ Do you reward or punish failure?

✓ How quickly does your marketing organization adopt change?

✓ How consistent is your customer experience across the company?

✓ What is the level of marketing's dependency on other departments?

3

Realigning Your Structure

From Silos to Convergence

Once your people have started to change their mind-set, the next thing to change is how your organization is structured, both within the marketing group and in interactions with other departments. The traditional view of a linear relationship with the customer no longer works. Marketing, sales, and customer service departments each had their own relationship with that customer. But because of the explosion in the number of channels that we use to communicate with our customers, and our customers' shifting expectations of how we interact with them, the old way of doing things isn't good enough anymore. Rather, we need to think about how we can conduct a far more cohesive conversation with our customers. They don't want to experience our silos.

One significant change in structure relates to marketing's adoption of all the new communication channels available in the digital space. Figure 3-1 depicts exactly how customers might view a channel focus compared to a customer focus.

FIGURE 3-1

From channel focus to customer focus

From . . .

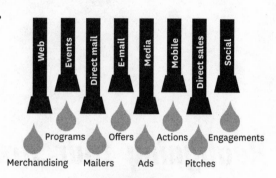

Programs   Offers   Actions   Engagements

Merchandising   Mailers   Ads   Pitches

To . . .

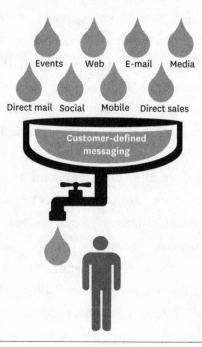

Events   Web   E-mail   Media

Direct mail   Social   Mobile   Direct sales

Customer-defined messaging

We have been adopting, testing, and investing in all these channels, and over time, we even organized our teams around the channels. Each time a new channel emerges, like e-mail or social media (blogs, Twitter, Facebook, and so on), we create a team—digital marketing team, search marketing team, social media team, e-mail marketing, for example—or assign responsibility to someone to manage it and connect to customers through it. We have gotten very good at reporting and measuring these channels. Defined testing strategies help us determine how a channel is performing and what levers we can adjust.

At some point, we started to see another shift. It became very obvious that while our channel performance effort was necessary and informative, all of these channels were starting to converge and were going to significantly change the way we evaluated and managed our investments. While it may seem obvious, we were effectively ignoring the idea of channel convergence (see figure 3-1), as all of marketing was busy testing new channels and forming new teams to manage the channels, especially across digital marketing, which encompassed areas such as:

- Website strategy

- E-commerce marketing

- Search engine marketing and optimization

- Social media marketing

- Social media monitoring and response

- Digital and social advertising

- Owned, earned, and paid digital communications (blogs, online publishing, and media)

- Online communities

- E-mail marketing and nurturing

- Online chat engines

- Content marketing elements such as syndication and deployment strategies

Effectively converging channels means engaging with the customer in one consistent voice. While all these channels are distinct, direct connection occurs between all the activities within each of them. The activities within a channel can affect another channel's results (both positively and negatively). We also realized that customers don't necessarily want to hear from us on every channel. What they want instead is that we communicate with them by their channel of choice. If we connected with a customer by, say, e-mail, he doesn't want us to force him into a different channel like social media or a direct phone call. This applies to both outbound conversations, which we initiate, and to inbound connections, which the customer initiates. The channel messaging also needs alignment. Content across channels is another element of coordination for achieving maximum amplification.

The trouble arose, then, when we failed to coordinate our communications across all the different channels we had open. We risked alienating our customers because we lost track of how we were connecting with them. No matter how creative or appealing the message, we realized we couldn't afford to broadcast it to indifferent or unlikely recipients. Get it wrong and we could be seen as noise, diminishing the return on our marketing investment while throwing money at people who simply tuned us out. We might send different campaigns to the same prospect or, worse, bombard them with messages they had no interest in whatsoever.

We once sent three hundred e-mails to a customer during an eighteen-day period. How did that happen? When I knew we needed to learn more about how to converge channels, I turned to key leadership to find the answers. Channels do not operate independently and neither should we, because they actually complement and improve each other's performance. Jennifer Chase, SAS senior marketing director, put it nicely when she said, "There are even times when you can draw the wrong conclusions when you look at the performance of a channel independently." For example, if someone says something negative about your company on Twitter, you might jump to conclusions about her level of engagement with the business. But Chase also said that focusing on a single channel might mean you miss out on the larger context for why a customer sent that tweet. "But it can also be very difficult to conduct an in-depth discussion with someone using 140 characters at a time," she said. The strategy therefore should be to encourage the customer to move the conversation elsewhere—maybe to e-mail, chat, or the phone—as a way to figure out the best way to resolve her problem. "Customer expectations have shifted," Chase told me. "They expect that you as a company know them and what actions they have already taken with you. They expect you to connect the dots."

The key point is that once you've made the switch to embrace an analytical mind-set, you'll need to make a series of internal structural changes to your organization to take advantage of those new capabilities. That all begins with altering how you look at and react to your customers. In short, you need to look at the forest as a whole instead of focusing on the trees alone. Our solution was to take a step back and evaluate where we had applied bandages and patches that were failing us. I took my leadership team offsite and asked them point blank: If we had the chance to start from scratch and rebuild our organization, what would it look like? How could we change our thinking to become more analytical and modern in interacting with our customers? How do we put customers at the center?

The answer was that we had to do a renovation and bring our channels together and create a new customer-centric view of the market.

We needed a way to monitor all of the different campaigns we might be running for a customer from a centralized place. We knew we had to create unified messaging across all of our channels and give our customers the kind of personalized attention they are asking for. And we did that by creating the framework depicted in figure 3-2.

In order to effectively manage a multichannel approach in digital, we realized that we needed to:

- Align investment strategies.

- Create more consistent messaging, content, and creative.

- Define rules of execution for those publishing content.

- Develop and monitor consistent performance metrics.

- Enforce continual internal communication.

- Align performance objectives across teams, creating interdependencies.

FIGURE 3-2

Analytical marketing functional framework

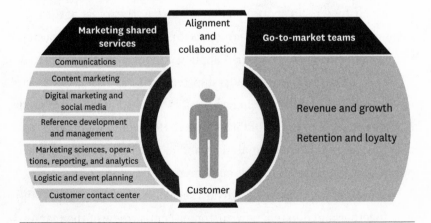

These kinds of changes were painful. People tended to focus on their area of expertise or influence at the exclusion of everything else. We were asking them to look at the bigger picture instead and understand the consequences when they undertook an action. In short, we needed to adopt a much more unified approach to how we thought about everything, from our campaigns to how we handled inbound contact from prospects.

After many iterations of organizational design, we landed on the framework shown in the figure. The framework served two purposes. It became the global structure for organizing marketing consistently in order to have maximum impact, improve communications, and optimize resources. The other purpose was to demonstrate a design that supports both a shared services approach and a go-to-market approach. We defined marketing shared services as those functions that could operate most effectively as a more centralized approach, leveraging channel expertise and establishing a service-level model. We also converged similar channels into these teams. In the go-to-market approach, everything comes together, resulting in a marketing plan aligned to our messages and driven by our customer knowledge. Marketing shared services and go-to-market teams have common objectives. The framework comes to life in slightly different ways, depending on the size or scope of a region, but our intent with the framework was to create a foundation from which to align, collaborate, and integrate our efforts as much as possible.

Going to Market—In a New Way

When we leverage the power of customer experience analytics, we can then understand all of the intersection and entry points we have with our customers—what I defined in a previous chapter as their "digital footprint." This digital footprint connects all sources of customer data interactions that tell a story of that individual or the company overall. For marketing, this type of information allows for increased targeting and segmentation, analyzing trends, and evaluating the performance of a particular site or asset. Marketing can apply scores and trigger actions as a way to design a better go-to-market plan, which is how we present ourselves to the external world in a cohesive and aligned way.

To get a more holistic view of the market beyond the limitations of any one channel, your marketing analytics strategy should allow you to fully capture all the data, apply visualization techniques, and create an outcome that marketers will be able to consume as they make decisions about campaigns, activities, and plans. The analytics and reporting empower better decision making to increase the rate of success in channel convergence. The impact of convergence flows into reorganizing modern marketing teams.

A key example of one such change we made as a marketing organization was to rethink how we implemented our go-to-market efforts, including all our campaigns and channels. In the past, for instance, we expected marketers to be experts in every aspect they needed to support a new campaign, from social media and content to lead generation and event preparation. They also had to know everything about the product or service around which they were building a campaign. They needed to be a jack-of-all-trades.

But that's now changed. Given the complexities and intricacies involved with all the different channels, let alone the rising importance of content as part of an effective campaign, it doesn't make sense for marketers to be good at everything. Rather, go-to-market leaders act more like the conductor of an orchestra: someone who both understands the expertise of the team members around her and knows how to pull them in at the moment they're needed to make the campaign a success. "The concept of the orchestrator evolved from the idea that it would be great to have someone who had a view of the entire organization and who could help connect the dots," said

Establishing a Go-to-Market Office

A go-to-market (GTM) office owns the definition, building, and orchestration of GTM programs and campaigns aligned to corporate initiatives.

Revenue and Growth Marketing

- Demand generation and pipeline marketing

- Client management, reference management, and development

Retention and Loyalty Marketing

- Current customer and adoption marketing

- User group support

- Education practice marketing and academic outreach programs

Country or Business Unit Go-to-Market Dimension

- Adopts, executes, and provides inputs for regionwide or global programs

- Owns the localization and customization of regionwide or global programs, and campaigns to the local markets

- Develops marketing strategy, programs, and campaigns unique to the country

- Is the primary interface to country sales and field organization

- Gives input to overall business and marketing process, including feedback

Scott Batchelor, a marketing manager whose team is charged with mounting the go-to-market campaigns for SAS analytics products. And as Felicia Ramsey, the marketing manager in charge of customer intelligence and risk solutions at SAS, noted, "In a digital marketing department, you need specialists and someone to bring them all together. The marketer will know their topic well, but they are also at the center of bringing in the right people to build the best go-to-market program."

An Orchestrator in Action

We use the term "orchestrator" to describe the job of marketers who make connections between different areas within our organization in order to bring a campaign to market. Their key functions are:

- Marketing around the customer decision journey for a key initiative.

- Synchronizing digital and traditional marketing channels so that SAS is found more often, more effectively, and by more customers.

- Ensuring the customer journey approach is progressing with key stakeholders.

- Engaging with client managers to identify needs for business units.

- Acting as point of contact for leadership and senior leadership across SAS.

- Ensuring alignment with sales targets and marketing strategy.

- Actively participating in product launches.

A marketing specialist who reports to Batchelor or Ramsey, for example, taps channel and product-specific experts from within the organization for help in building a campaign, but also accesses resources like our external communications team and PR teams as well as our corporate creative team, which serves as our in-house creative resource. Figure 3-3 shows how all the components of a go-to-market plan combine. The marketer orchestrator sits at the middle, bringing together all those different levels of expertise. According to Chase, "The goal is to create a plan that is aligned internally and externally, and that takes a multichannel approach and is anchored by the customer journey."

FIGURE 3-3

Go-to-market framework

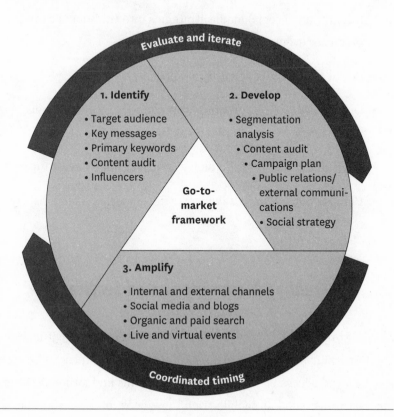

When you're managing many campaigns, knowing who you're sending information to or who you're expecting results from is critical to your success. When you optimize those efforts, score the data, and put models in place that give you more information about behaviors and interactions, you will see immediate impact in the form of cost savings and campaign effectiveness. For instance, we experienced a reduction in e-mail opt-outs by about 20 percent and increased click-through rates by about 30 percent. Because the campaign is highly optimized, we're getting the right information to the right people. So the results are higher-quality leads, reduced costs, and a better experience for our customers.

Some examples of channel convergence in action include:

- Back links in blog posts to increase search volume.

- Integration of social media strategies into traditional campaigns or events.

- Social media sharing within advertising.

- Optimization of search word strategies across all channels consistently.

- Incorporation of chat technology within e-mail marketing.

- Consistency in *all* digital advertising—search, social, display, network, and more.

Creating Marketing Shared Services

Another area where we needed convergence was in content marketing. Content has become a critical part of marketing and must be both relevant and accessible in many different forms and for many different platforms, such as mobile-friendly, videos, ebooks, slideshows, and so on. It's not enough to post white papers on your site for customers to download.

The trouble arises, though, in generating content. Or, more specifically, making sure there is coordination across the organization for acquiring it. We found that we had different channels investing time and money in acquiring content, such as by hiring someone to write a research paper, when another department channel already had a similar paper sitting in its archives. We were continually reinventing the wheel and wasting plenty of money, because we weren't coordinating our efforts. "We were the worst offenders of creating random acts of content," said Barbara Anthony, who has worked for SAS for twenty-eight years and is now the director of the digital and content marketing team.

Our solution was to create a shared service called content marketing that would be a central resource every campaign or go-to-market team could coordinate with when acquiring or sharing content, as well as a content framework to show the connection of content creation and marketing (see figure 3-4).

Anthony leads the team that created a catalog and inventory of our existing content. They then scored each piece of content based on its effectiveness. John Balla, a content marketer, was a member of the six-person team that reviewed every single piece of content we had in-house. Balla had been working at SAS for eight years as a campaign team lead and content creator, blogging, contracting research, and recording event content to promote in digital formats. In his new role, his focus is to evaluate existing content inventory and guide content development to improve campaign performance and other forms of audience engagement, such as search and social media. As an example, Balla and his team reviewed every white paper the company had collectively written about the subject of data management. They also watched every video and webinar we had filmed and then judged each piece with a figurative thumbs-up or thumbs-down. "We were looking for the pieces that were the most consistent with the story we're trying to tell as a company,"

Implementing Marketing Shared Services

We have rethought our structure by redefining those components in our organization that would be optimized by establishing a shared service—globally or regionally.

Content and Communication Services

- Content planning, procurement, and placement (deploy and amplify)

- Content curating and management

- Reference management

- External communications and analyst relations

- Multilanguage delivery

Digital and Creative Marketing Services

- Digital advertising (display, search, etc.)

- Creative design for all channels

- Social media marketing

- Website and e-commerce marketing

- Search engine optimization

- Emerging channels

Balla told me. For instance, he said he had read some 127 white papers on the topic of data management alone, 62 of which passed muster.

One approach Balla uses to screen the content is quantitative; he assigns each asset a score based on its search term keyword density.

Marketing Sciences, Analytics, and Reporting Services

- Systems, process, and governance

- Metrics, reporting, and analytics

- Marketing automation (including e-mail marketing)

- Data strategy (including nurturing and segmentation)

- Lead management

- Marketing operations, forecasting, budgeting

Event Planning and Logistics Services

- Plan for event project management systems and processes

- Create and execute pan-regional events

Customer Contact Center

- Inbound focus customer experience and service

- Demand generation

- Social media monitoring and response

- Multichannel (chat, phone, e-mail, web, social)

In that way, he evaluates whether the author uses the same words and phrases that customers use in Internet browsers during the different stages of their decision journey. While objective, that approach doesn't provide a complete evaluation of the content. Balla also told

FIGURE 3-4

Content framework

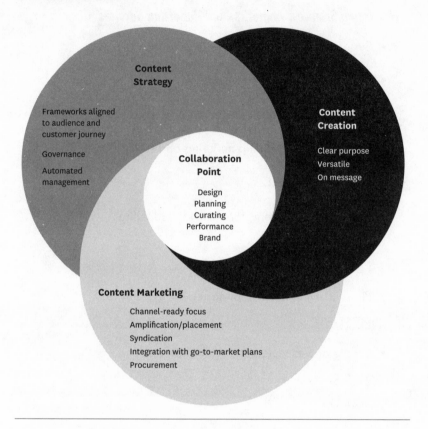

me that some subjective scoring is needed because search perfor-mance is only part of the picture. White papers are evaluated for the quality of writing as well. "We have to remember that we are deal-ing with human beings who are reading something," he said. "So we scored content based on whether it was well written or just stale and mismatched with expectations set by the asset title."

Another result of our content review process was that we uncovered gaps, target areas where we didn't have enough or any content. "We may have had tons of white papers on the subject of the customer journey," Anthony explained, "but maybe we needed an ROI calculator as well."

At the same time, we posed a challenge to marketers—they needed to evolve from thinking only of managing their specific channels into becoming orchestrators, someone who uses the data and analytics to test and understand different strategies that are most effective with our customers and prospects. "To successfully manage our relationships with the customer," Anthony told me, "we learned that we had to centralize our operations."

Developing New Department Relationships

The seeds for the structural changes to implement our analytical approach to marketing began in 2007, when terms like social media and Web 2.0 were becoming mainstream. An enormous shift was occurring in the digital world, and the leaders of the various marketing departments created an internal group called the Marketing 2.0 Council to talk through and digest the major implications these changes might have on our organizations.

Those council meetings were very successful and helped us promote our brand through the new emerging channels and to better coordinate how we could leverage outlets like blogs, YouTube, Twitter, and the rest for both outbound and inbound communications with our customers.

As the complexity of the digital communications world continued to proliferate, we as an organization realized that it wasn't just marketing that was affected by the changes in technology and how people used it. Our entire organization had to adjust. That sparked the creation of a new council we dubbed "Digitize the Business." We included representatives from almost every department in the company. Our goal was to collaborate on modernizing and enhancing our customers' experiences with us. As Aaron Hill, one of the key drivers and coordinators of the Digitize the Business efforts, told me, "We needed to start sharing these digital things we were doing with marketing across the company because it was now impacting all of us. We needed to start collaborating and working together." That meant that as a marketing organization, we had to rethink our relationships with other departments in the company and understand how analytics could help us work more closely together. The foundation for those changes began with developing a strong partnership with our IT department.

Partnering with IT

Marketing technology continues to grow and change, which is both overwhelming and exciting. Regardless of how amazing the technology or tool may be, I like to say that "the devil is in the data." That's why a marketing analytics strategy requires constant care and feeding of the data, and that the integration, management, and governance of the data must remain a constant priority.

Given the complexity of the technology landscape, the ability to focus on which areas demand attention and prioritize investments and implementations is essential. Modern marketing organizations, therefore, need to implement a technology road map that delivers automation, empowers the marketers directly, and incorporates a data-driven priority. But embracing the technology for handling that data presents a challenge for marketing. While marketing requires new technical skills (more on that in the next chapter), we're not the experts when it comes to the technology. Now that we are relying so heavily on data and analytical tools to do our work, we need more help from experts in how we can both create and collect enterprise-level customer data, while also ensuring its integrity. Without good, clean data, we can't market very well, no matter how sophisticated our tools are.

In the past, marketing might have developed its own tools and databases to house the information collected. We would go out and buy our own hardware and software to get up and running quickly. We recognized that not only was this going to duplicate resources within our organization, but we simply didn't have the in-house expertise to maintain the systems. We had to have the IT team as our partner instead. We recognized that we needed IT for its expertise in storing, integrating, modeling, and providing a consistent structure for our data.

At the same time, IT had to have our understanding of the business needs to know what questions to ask when capturing the most important data. This relationship can't be neglected, because as customers change, marketing changes, and the channels of engagement morph and data explodes. Ultimately, the partnership between IT and marketing will be the linchpin for new, emerging opportunities. Today, our marketing organization has a great partnership with the IT department. But it wasn't always that way. The relationship wasn't bad, just static.

Fortunately for us, Berni Mobley, SAS senior vice president of IT, was very open and proactive about the idea of her department becoming a business partner with marketing. Similarly, she also began to change the mind-set of the people in the IT department, helping them shift from thinking only of features and functions and more about our business objectives with the systems we put in place. Mobley and her team recognized that, in order to take advantage of new channels and data, they had to interact differently with marketing.

Traditional back-office IT—responding to issues, maintaining infrastructure, and considering only internal customers—wasn't going to cut it. The new IT department is strategic, targeting the same customers as marketing. Not only do the IT people attend marketing meetings, they participate strategically, advising marketing at planning stages. No longer does the marketing department send requests to IT after finishing planning and hoping resources are available. "Being involved with marketing up front and hearing their business needs helps IT be more proactive in allocating resources and suggesting new technologies to help them reach their goals sooner," Mobley told me. "As their partner, when marketing succeeds, my staff feels proud of the role they played and that fosters the desire to do it again."

For example, when we undertook the effort to completely overhaul the SAS.com website, we worked with Mobley as cosponsors of the project to ensure that the site was not going to be merely informational, but that it would also have e-commerce capabilities and that its primary goal would be to create a different online experience for our customers.

Mobley even created a new position, an integration analyst, to help formalize the partnership between marketing and IT. The integration analyst is present at the outset of any marketing initiative to ensure marketing needs are met using the latest technologies that fit into the IT infrastructure. Instead of saying something like, "No, you'll create technical issues," when we talk about a potential new project, IT now says things like, "Here's a cool new application that will fix that problem."

To further solidify our partnership, IT and marketing both participated in hiring the best candidate to fill the integration analyst role, because we wanted someone who had technology chops and could speak the language of business. As Mobley explained to me, "It was very important to me that it was a joint decision on who to hire for this position. The integration analyst position benefits both IT and marketing. IT gains a much deeper understanding of the business and acts as a communication bridge between the two departments, which ultimately helps IT deliver a better product for marketing."

Even though we now hire marketers with very technical skill sets, we are not competing with IT. The people we are hiring are using their skills to dig deeply into the data the IT folks maintain in a very complementary relationship.

Many organizations see IT, like marketing, as a cost center rather than a source of revenue. But, by partnering with us when supporting our analytical backbone, we can begin to share a story of how we jointly contribute to the bottom line.

This concept also applies to the continued analytical transformation in our global offices. As we undergo modernization efforts internationally, we already have the partnership with IT in place that allows us to debate and collaborate on the best solution for the entire organization.

We've evolved our system of record to be a true marketing analytics portal. Analytics, the reporting, the graphics, and our understanding of the trends have enabled campaign teams working with the sales organization to fully demonstrate value. Our marketing analytics portal is connected to all the systems and to a single view of the data. Building that portal and empowering people with data and analysis are critical components to delivering results, and ultimately to our credibility. But we couldn't have done it without IT support—data management, hosting, training, troubleshooting, and all the other ways it has supported us.

Establishing a deeper partnership between IT and marketing can take time, so enter this transition with patience. For example, James Weber, chief marketing officer and executive vice president at Comerica Bank, explained that at first, he didn't have a collaborative relationship with his chief information officer (CIO). But after the CIO retired, and with the help of an outside consultant, Weber said that his organization recognized that it needed to look at IT as a teammate rather than an obstacle, especially because the organization's outdated data architecture prevented marketing from effectively mining data. "We can't continue to do things the traditional way anymore," he told me. "We need the ability to go in and mine the data, take insight to another level, and find the opportunities, especially when thinking about your own customer base. This impacts the customer experience."

To help overcome those barriers, IT and marketing at Comerica came together to sponsor a data governance council to consolidate how the company was managing data across its different functional silos. "We didn't have a data architecture, data standards, or governance," Weber explained. "It was being done in pockets. Some business units were skeptical that they would lose control of how they thought things needed to be done. It took time, but we broke through that."

Using Analytics to Bridge the Sales Gap

Another internal structural change we've undergone as a result of our marketing modernization efforts is to cement our relationship with the sales department. The sales and marketing relationship needs constant care and feeding. It must be deliberate, measurable, and aligned.

While sales and marketing groups historically approach initiatives from different directions, they can use a common language (like leads, sales, retention, or loyalty) to maintain a constant dialogue and find new strategies that can lead to more sales. For SAS sales and marketing groups, there were huge amounts of data on the activity of a contact. Systems tracked a person from initial capture as a lead through his interactions with the website, events, and other campaigns. As in any company, though, there was often confusion about what the data meant and how the two groups interpreted the effectiveness of marketing efforts.

A typical challenge for the SAS marketing group was communicating the overall impact of outreach efforts. When they met, our sales counterparts wanted to know:

- How did different marketing channels perform?

- What types of interactions provided the best outcomes?

- Which assets were the most effective when engaging with the customer?

As an analytics company that develops dashboards, scorecards, and other business intelligence tools, SAS had long been ahead of the curve in working with marketing data. Still, many of the reports were based on outdated structures or cumbersome data schemes, and, as a result, teams (on both sides) found it difficult to access the data they needed.

This problem intensified at the executive level. Confusion at lower levels about the performance of activities made it more difficult to provide reports to sales and marketing executives. This compromised our ability to put the right amount of resources behind high-performing programs, especially if it was unclear which programs were, in fact, performing well.

We began the process of collaborating better by learning to speak a common language in which we could show salespeople the kind of digital and analytical information they needed to land new accounts. By relying on our marketing and analytical information, we could bring real, actionable information via the customer's digital footprint to the salespeople, which was like handing them the Holy Grail.

The sales organization talks numbers, so we as marketers need to talk numbers. All our efforts and investments are also now aligned to the sales organization's objectives and targets. A sales organization has a revenue number and a set of metrics related to customer retention. In turn, we measure the success of our marketing efforts based on the impact we have on building a sales pipeline, driving revenue, and influencing renewals. Our metrics include many of the traditional marketing assessments, but with a clear focus on how we are affecting the pipeline revenue for our overall business. We also provide the sales organization with a view into those results at contact and company levels. We can clearly define and measure impact at the bottom line.

Marketing Analytics at Work

Scoring Leads to Drive More Effective Sales

Leads are the lifeblood of any sales effort. But, not all leads are created equal. Some have a high value for an organization and represent a realistic opportunity to win business. Others are early-stage engagements that take months or years of development for a sales opportunity.

Because of this disparity, the question of "what is a lead?" puzzles many organizations. Sales and marketing groups have worked for years to formalize the definition of a lead and what it means within an existing business model. Regardless of your definition, one thing is consistent: marketing has to adapt its strategies to bring in more, better, or just different mixes of leads. The key question is, how do you get there?

The Challenge

Over the years, the SAS marketing organization built a complex method of passing leads from marketing to sales. The process was similar to what other companies have in place, that is, leads that met a set of rules were qualified and then sent to a salesperson to follow up. The system was effective but difficult to manage, especially when business needs changed.

To build a new model to score and qualify leads, the marketing team looked at existing data and then conferred with their counterparts in sales to reorient the lead management process to accomplish two main goals:

1. *Increase the number and percentage of leads that convert to opportunities.* This meant identifying the best leads and finding a faster way to pass more high-qualified leads to sales.

2. *Improve the outcomes from the lead conversion process.* Obviously, high-quality leads are essential to creating a larger pipeline of deals. The team needed a better way to score and then prioritize leads.

An added wrinkle was that the project had to be global, so a lead in Australia, for example, would have the same meaning as a lead in Germany. That way, the company could compare lead performance across geographies and fuel global decisions about what strategies would be more effective.

The Approach

While the previous rules-based model was geared more toward quantity, the team opted for a model-based approach to lead scoring that emphasized quality based on likely outcomes. The team developed an analytics-driven model that could evaluate the range of customer behaviors (registrations, website page views, e-mail clicks, and so on) to identify the best leads.

Beyond the quality-versus-quantity discussion, the sales and marketing teams agreed that the timing of the lead handoff to sales was also important. To accomplish this effectively, the model evaluated many behaviors, and once certain criteria were met, the information was added to the customer relationship management (CRM) system.

To improve the lead conversion process, the team also focused on converting more sales-ready leads. Not only did the new scoring model evaluate more behavioral data, but that information was passed on as a "digital footprint" for each lead. The salesperson now sees the interactions for the lead from within the CRM system, giving her important information to guide her initial outreach.

Additionally, the team decided not to send all leads to the CRM system. Since the model does a better job of classifying better leads, those that aren't routed to sales go to a lead-nurturing program, where the contact receives a cadence of relevant e-mails. The contact's behavior when receiving those e-mails (click-throughs, registrations, website visits, and so on) are all fed into the model.

The Results

When the lead scoring model was still in the early stages, the initial feedback was positive. Salespeople appreciated that the leads they were seeing were more qualified and reliable. Rather than sifting through dozens of contacts, they know that leads have demonstrated an interest in SAS and its solutions. That was once a luxury for a salesperson; now, it's an everyday reality.

To fine-tune the model, analysts track the overall number of leads passed to sales and the number that convert to opportunities. The marketing team wants to make sure the rates continue to rise for both numbers. If there is a plateau or a decline, the analysts receive rapid feedback and can adjust programs as necessary.

SAS marketing analysts can also fine-tune the model as sales requirements change or the market evolves. The model is more flexible than the rules-based approach, allowing the team to adjust strategies rapidly. The team can adjust the lead conversion rate if there is a shift in internal focus or if a sales group has more or less capacity.

FIGURE 3-5

Lead distribution across segments screenshot

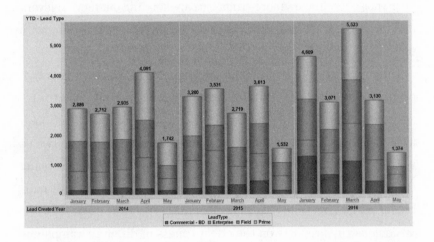

The report in figure 3-5 gives an example of the types of information available for sales and marketing. The chart shows leads created across different groups (commercial, enterprise, and field sales teams) from year to year. In simplest terms, the team can look at this to evaluate areas that are lacking in leads and where to focus in the future. It can then drill into more detailed reports to find the story behind the numbers.

The sales and marketing teams now use these reports to find opportunities for growth based on the past behavior of customers and the collective performance of campaigns already run. The data is now accessible by stakeholders, and this information can serve as a starting point for both strategic and tactical discussions. Together, we utilize this information to make decisions and adjustments as needed. "There's an old adage that says, with marketing, we knew that 50 percent of what we did was working," said Gene Gsell, vice president of retail and consumer packaged goods at SAS. "We just didn't know which half was actually working. That was the world we used to live in. It was all based on getting marketing to get us the maximum number of eyeballs. But everything is different today. We're not guessing anymore. Today we are sending out more relevant and targeted information that has created a real feedback loop with our customers. We now know what works and what doesn't."

One big step we took to facilitate the kinds of conversations that ensure alignment between sales and our marketing team was to create a new position in the marketing organization called "client manager." Amanda Thomas, who has been working at SAS for twelve years, stepped up to take this role, which she described as "being that conduit between sales and marketing. My job is to look at marketing campaigns from a sales perspective."

Thomas runs reports on the effectiveness of different campaigns we are supporting; she can slice and dice the data and results by business unit, territory, and even down to the granular level of each sales rep. She can then identify the key prospect leads that we are generated for the sales pipeline by those campaigns and then communicate those to the sales team members so they can see the best opportunities for investing their resources. Thomas then attends weekly and monthly meetings with different representatives of the sales team to help them understand where various customers might be on their decision journeys and what sales might do to interact with them more effectively. "Amanda participates in our meetings and gets the heartbeat of what we're doing," said David Macdonald, vice president of sales and financial services. "She can then feed to the marketing team what's most interesting and exciting. Similarly, she helps us understand something like our upcoming company event schedule and which ones might be the best for us to make our own investments in, based on the potential fit of the attendees for our products."

For example, she was reviewing the reports that showed which clients had the best response to the marketing campaigns run over the past eighteen months. When the sales team members then showed their follow-ups during that same period, Thomas saw something they had overlooked. While salespeople had been aggressively following up on clients who showed interest in solutions related to customer intelligence software, Thomas noticed they hadn't realized that many of those same prospects were also searching simultaneously for data management as well. Thomas was able to take a deeper look at the digital footprint those different prospects were leaving behind. Bringing that kind of analytical muscle to meetings has greatly expanded the level of trust that sales now places in marketing, because we can now report tangible results and not just anecdotal evidence about how a campaign is reporting. "And we can share that information with sales in real time," Thomas told me, "which means we can help them follow up on the best leads faster."

With Thomas's help, we also began to educate sales on the power of "social selling," the idea of connecting to people via the vast number of social media channels, using the information in our customer's digital footprints. This took some adjustment, because the world of sales has changed as well. Cold calls no longer make sense. Why would you invest your time and energy in such an inefficient process when, by using the information from a prospect's digital footprint, you can multiply your productivity and effectiveness by a hundredfold? Gone are the days when you could only market to someone face-to-face at a trade show, when you might be able to land ten names for your pipeline. Today, we can create a list of ten thousand high-quality prospects at virtually no cost, which serves to greatly increase the effectiveness of a sales rep.

Gene Gsell admits that the relationship between sales and marketing continues to evolve, but it will keep improving over time as he and Thomas help educate the team about the new realities of the customer journey. "Culturally, it has been a somewhat difficult transition for the sales organization," Gsell said. "Initially, we had people on our team saying that when they conducted online searches on certain keywords they thought were critical and SAS didn't show up in the results, they were upset. But when we talked to marketing and found out that the analytics proved that no one was actually using those terms, we could all get on the same page. The data helps us avoid making the kinds of assumptions we did in the past, while also saving us wasted time and energy chasing things that wouldn't help us achieve our shared goals."

When we began to have conversations like this with the sales team members, we started to build their trust and respect for how the power of marketing analytics could actually make them into more effective salespeople. Similarly, our tools could help them retain their existing customers and identify other opportunities to expand those relationships. "The analytics can help lead us to better places and better decisions," Gsell said. "Where emotion used to carry the day, we can now rely on much more informed opinions."

Show Finance the Money

The more we as marketers are able to affect the bottom line, the better our relationship with the finance department becomes as well. The fact that we can now use data and analytics to track our activities—to show where we spent money and what the resulting impact was—is music to a finance person's ears. By doing this, we can change the kinds of conversations we have traditionally had around budgets, because we no longer only justify why we need a certain amount: we have the numbers, the results, and outcomes to show the finance people. That's helped shift their mind-set from thinking of marketing solely as a cost center.

To help build the communications between our departments, we have a dedicated liaison with finance for budgeting and expenses. Linda Hester works with me every quarter to generate reports, using our own software, that demonstrate the impact of our marketing efforts on revenue and on the growth of the sales pipeline. "By providing that kind of data, we are completely transparent," Hester told me. "That has helped us establish a level of trust and respect that goes a long way. We have helped finance understand that marketing doesn't just spend money recklessly, but that there are goals and outcomes that result from the money we do spend."

Hester said that one key result of that greater understanding of how marketing can actually prove the ROI of its budget is that, unlike every other organization she has worked in, marketing can propose its budget each quarter, rather than have finance give a fixed amount. Hester continued, "We've been able to move past the 'spend it or lose it' mentality into having much more of a conversation. Finance is much more flexible because they trust us more."

Another result of this improved communication and collaboration is that we now have finance folks coming to us and asking what kinds of reports they can provide *us* that would help our efforts. And it's all because of the power of data and analytics. You might even ask yourself, what other kinds of interdepartmental relationships can you change in your organization using those same tools?

Going Global?

Another recent change is in the concept of using analytics to create more unified marketing globally. Now, other organizations are likely further ahead of us in this area. But SAS as an organization has been based on the idea of creating geography-specific teams and campaigns. Patrick Xhonneux, for example, headed up marketing for five countries in Europe—Portugal, Spain, France, the Netherlands, and Belgium. He said that until a few years ago, he treated the markets in each of those countries as silos, where campaigns would be budgeted, built, and targeted to the customers based there. But that's all changed. "We recognize that the world is becoming flat and that there are no national borders anymore in the digital worlds," Xhonneux explained to me. "All customers are now global. That means we need to change and understand their needs."

What Xhonneux, who is in charge of marketing for all of Europe, the Middle East, and Africa, came to understand was that treating countries as their own silos was no longer good enough; he needed to craft campaigns that could cross all of them, with some degree of customization to account for language and cultural differences added in. The priority was to ensure that there was a consistent message from SAS, regardless of what country customers were in or what language they were doing their research in. A customer could attend an event in one country, for example, but actually be based in another country. If we didn't have a consistent message or way to nurture that prospect, we could miss out on turning him into a lead and, eventually, a customer.

To push that dynamic forward, Xhonneux restructured his organization; he created shared services that campaign teams across the continent could access. Not only did that reorganization create new efficiencies on the back end by ensuring that people weren't duplicating their efforts, it also helped to ensure the consistency of messages and content that was lacking before. Just three months later, conversion rates skyrocketed across all five countries. Xhonneux explained, "One key of modern marketing is that you need to continually reinvent yourself, because things continue to change so fast. This now begs the question of how much further can we go? We are asking ourselves if we can add more countries to our region. Is there a limit?"

Cameron Dow, the vice president of marketing who oversees Canada and Latin America, agrees that the dynamics of the digital age have transformed how marketing organizations need to be structured. "The advent of digital communications has broken down barriers and walls," he said. "We were traditionally organized by business unit and country. But those borders are thin now." When it comes to social media influencers, for example, Dow told me that it's no longer practical or even wise to think about simply targeting people based solely on their geography: "We need to think more about coordinating on a global basis."

That said, going global with a unified approach to campaigns brings challenges as well. If we wanted to build a global campaign around a digital piece of property like an ebook, for example, would it be enough to simply translate it into twenty-five languages and push it out? "It might not be the right asset for every region," Xhonneux explained. "It might be that one-size-fits-all may not be the best approach. I think it will come down to finding that balance between strategy and execution." Dow agrees, especially because different markets have different adoption levels for technology and digital devices. He told me that, in the end, the priority is to remain agile and flexible with regard to what our customers are telling us. "We can't become wedded to any one strategy if we're not focused on trying to create value for the company as a whole," Dow said.

Now that we have thought through some of the structural changes you will need to make in your organization, let's turn now to the people you will need to cultivate and the positions they will hold.

When Was the Last Time You Really Changed the Marketing Structure Itself?

What does your organizational structure look like, both within marketing and outside of it? Ask yourself whether the silos you have inside marketing are efficient and whether they might be preventing you from maximizing your limited resources. Do you really need separate teams for different channels or even products? There are no right or wrong answers. But consider how you might uncover more efficiency if you took a fresh look at your structure.

Similarly, what do the relationships with other departments in your organization look like? Are there ways you can bridge the gaps and change the kinds of conversations you have with, say, sales and IT? Are there ways you can create new partnerships with your peers there? The key takeaway here is to assess how you can rethink the role that marketing plays in your organization so that you can show the true value of your team's efforts to the company's bottom line.

To assess your organization's structure, take your leadership team offsite for at least two days and go through the following exercise:

✓ If you could design a modern analytical marketing organization from scratch, what would it look like?

✓ Define the primary objectives (goals) for this modern marketing organization.

✓ List all the functions that should be in marketing (*not* the current picture, but what it should be).

   – Identify functional dependencies.

   – Define intersection points across functions.

✓ Prioritize the functional areas. Gain agreement; it is important for everyone to be on the same page.

✓ Use the resulting information to design a functional view of marketing, not an organization chart (see figure 3-2). Again, gain agreement.

✓ Finally, use this newly defined functional view as your template for redesigning the current organization.

  – Identify areas of strength.

  – Identify gaps in skill sets, investment, and so on.

  – Determine the necessary staffing or business model (that is, outsourcing).

  – Document a way forward.

✓ The leadership team, the objectives, and this functional view become your guiding coalition for change and drive the vision forward. The coalition will provide you, as the leadership team, with both alignment and an acid test for staying on track.

✓ You will make mistakes along the way, and you can make adjustments; if you don't make mistakes, then you should be worried.

4

Building Talent and Skills

From Traditional to Modern

Once you've assessed the mind-set of the people in your organization and have thought through some of the structural changes you'll make, you need to think about *who* belongs in your marketing organization. Who's in? Who's out? What new positions should you create to optimize analytics? We turn to this topic next.

As you shift your organization to be both more analytical and customer-centric, you need to ensure that your people have the requisite skills to perform in the new kinds of roles you're creating. And that takes two components: incorporating a different filter for hiring new employees, and also assessing your current staff to see if they have the desire and capability to evolve and embrace the new analytical skills they'll need. "We know that pure data people rely more on the left side of their brains, while more classically trained marketers are more right-brained," according to Jennifer Chase, senior marketing director. "Building the analytically driven marketing organization is all about bringing the left and right sides of our brains together. You may excel at one side of your brain more than the other, but need to have an appreciation for both."

What Does An Analytical Marketer Look Like?

Marketing managers must look for evidence of *different* skills and experience in evaluating both applicants and current employees interested in becoming analytical marketers. But *what* to look for is open to debate. Here are some thoughts:

1. *Sales skills.* It's no longer good enough for marketing to simply focus on filling the top of the funnel and passing leads off to sales. The analytical marketer needs to be active throughout the buying process and work hand in hand with salespeople to provide the information that will help them close deals.

2. *Social media skills.* Social media dramatically change the buyer-seller-influencer dynamic. But only those actively participating in social media tangibly appreciate the differences between old-style, one-way media conversations and group interactivity.

3. *Journalism and storytelling skills.* With buyers getting the majority of their information from the web, and with potential sales an increasing priority, there's no end to the need for juicy, targeted content. Storytelling also comes into play in campaign design.

4. *Process design skills.* Automation is just beginning to penetrate the market. As anyone who has been part of a reengineering effort can attest, it's not the automation that increases

productivity. It's the process changes that automation enables and enforces. Deploying marketing automation will require skills such as process modeling, project management, the ability to train and manage change, and ease with technology.

5. *Data and analytics skills.* Technology captures and makes available enormous amounts of data about buyer and seller behavior. A marketer must be a data guru with a passion for analytics and curiosity. (I'll get into more detail about these skills later in the chapter.)

6. *Domain expertise.* Customers don't care about our products. They care about themselves and their problems. Building a bridge between our products and the customer requires knowledge of both realms.

7. *Collaboration* and *exceptional communication.* These skills are not mutually exclusive. On just about every job posting these days, you will see that "communication" skills are a must. Communication has a different meaning for marketers in our world. Traditional communication skills need to be supplemented with an intense focus on collaboration through effective communication. There are no one-man or -woman bands, only full orchestras with very clear objectives and constant interaction.

8. *Creativity and innovation.* We need people to reach for the next idea. The term "creativity" is no longer applicable to just the agencies or the designers. Today's channels and digital work approaches enable and encourage creativity at all stages of marketing and the marketing process. Creativity is at the heart of innovation, which is not only required but rewarded.

The New Analytical Marketers

With the foundation for a modern marketing organization in place, new roles have emerged:

- Client managers

    - Can be advocate, communicator, and marketer.

    - Bridge to business unit and internal clients.

- Orchestrators

    - Can lead complex go-to-market efforts and assure alignment.

    - Bridge to the external voice of SAS.

- Marketing data scientists or data visualization analysts or data storytellers

    - Can uncover the data and analytical stories.

    - Bridge to the data and analytics.

---

9. *Leadership.* A leader is someone who is willing to take risks, drive change, and build trust. We need these skills at every level of the organization, not just the vice president level. Today's marketers, regardless of their role, have a unique opportunity to demonstrate leadership in their field and across their business for maximum impact.

While far from exhaustive, this list of skills confirms that we are no longer looking only for traditional marketing skills. Marketing managers need evidence that candidates or existing employees bring different skills and experiences. Good analytical marketers leave a well-lit trail to make sure such evidence is easy to find.

- Segmentation analyst

  - Can see patterns and trends in behavior.

  - Bridge to the campaigns.

- IT business partners

  - Can relate business concepts to technology solutions.

  - Bridge between IT and marketing.

- Customer engagement specialists

  - Can create amazing customer experiences.

  - Bridge to the customer or prospect.

- Content marketer

  - Can bring content to life.

  - Bridge to the best content.

But to evolve into an analytical marketing organization, marketers today need to be more like scientists than artists, according to Phil Brojan of RCI. This requirement has changed how his organization thinks about hiring new marketers. "We now look for scientific and analytical skills and pick and choose where we put creative," he told me, while noting that finding and evaluating people with these skill sets can be difficult. "You have to have the right players in the right positions. Hire as much relevant experience as you can and mix that in with the folks that understand the business really well."

Regardless of the role someone plays in marketing, the expectations related to data and analytics should be consistent. While there will always be more advanced analytical and technical positions, there is a new baseline for all marketers. The skill set includes knowledge of data management principles and analytical strategies, and an understanding of the role of data quality, the importance of data governance, and the value of data in marketing disciplines. Today's marketer needs to go well beyond reporting and metrics, and be more proficient in a full range of analytics, which may include optimization, text, sentiment, scoring, modeling, visualization, forecasting, and attribution.

Marketers should have experience with the technology, tools, and design approaches that leverage data and analytics. Campaign design, multichannel integration, content performance, personalization, and digital marketing can all be driven by fact-based decision making, ideally with direct accountability to results and the ability to very quickly react and adjust to the demands of the customer and the market. The marketers I am referring to have a distinct blend of creativity and reasoning talents; they are inquisitive, inventive, and enthused by a culture that is advanced and agile.

As our functional needs have changed, we've had to adjust the kinds of jobs and job descriptions of people throughout our marketing organization. The emergence of data science combined with the proliferation of new channels has radically changed some traditional marketing jobs, while also leading to the creation of brand-new roles and titles. As a whole, all these changes are part of the evolution away from marketing simply as art into a hybrid of art and science. As a result, we've redefined four new categories or job families:

- Digital marketing

- Content marketing

- Marketing science

- Customer experience

Digital Marketing

The world of digital marketing includes the functions of web, search, social media, e-mail, and digital advertising and media buying. This category has been going through tremendous growth and change over the past decade as the number of channels has exploded. Consider how the job of someone like Elizabeth Creech, a SAS digital marketer involved in our paid search and display advertising efforts, has changed as advertising has shifted from print publications to digital. In the print world, it was difficult, if not impossible, to know if you were reaching your intended audience. Creech's job is now much more precise, thanks to analytics. As Creech said, "The transition to digital has made it much more likely that we can target the right person, at the right time, on the right device. We can also see what the world is looking at, based on keyword prices and search volumes. You can't fool digital like you could with print."

As the number of digital channels grew, our reaction was to continue to add channel specialists who could learn every nuance of how that channel operated in a way that allowed us to get closer to our customers. Consider how complicated it has become to orchestrate organic search result placement or people who can manage the daily investments required to make an effective paid search campaign relevant to the customer's decision journey. Similar dynamics apply to the rapidly shifting social media realm. We need to constantly add people who can drill down and drive communication through every new channel.

But what we've learned is that the real opportunity is in convergence and in creating strategies that leverage multiple channels rather than silos (as discussed in chapter 3). The result of that shift is that we now require multiple skill sets from each of our team members so that they can maintain excellence in their channels, but also understand the importance of coordinating with other components in a campaign as well. Put another way, we still have a need for skills that are narrow in one sense, but we also have to have people who can connect those skills to a broader view of where we're going as an organization to meet our goals. We can't have someone so focused on his one social channel, for example, that he doesn't recognize he is cannibalizing another one at the same time. That's counterproductive, because we are not serving our customers by doing that.

We're looking for people who are both passionate about their channel but also understand how it intersects with others. We need marketers who are capable of collaborating and who prioritize connection points while also using the data to guide them.

For example, before he recently transitioned into a new role as a segmentation analyst, Scott Sellers was one of our go-to resources for tapping into the world of online advertising and paid search. Sellers was responsible for helping the team understand where the best opportunities were for, say, purchasing keywords that our potential customers were most interested in getting information on. Sellers told me that his job was not unlike that of a police investigator who simply wanted to uncover the truth, rather than to prove any particular outcome for a potential campaign. "From an analytical standpoint, we need to be impartial with regards to the final outcome or decision," he said. "The key is to show people how you reached a conclusion based on your interpretation of the data. Someone else might reach a different conclusion, but at least we have something objective to talk about. Ideally you want every outcome to be perfect, but nobody is an oracle."

When Sellers and I discussed some of his experiences, he recalled that when he was involved in supporting paid search advertising, a campaign he was analyzing was using some very expensive search terms related to customer intelligence, which meant that our company wasn't alone in believing there was value in associating our brand with the campaign. That alone seemed like justification for keeping the campaign alive, since our goal was to engage with customers on their decision journey, wherever that might begin. But in our analytical era, making those kinds of assumptions simply doesn't suffice anymore. "It's all too common when you have a target market that you decide what you will focus on," Sellers explained. "You then look around your organization at the structures in place and decide to align your strategies, messaging, and campaigns along those internally created lines. The major problem with this approach is that it focuses on company thinking and ignores the behavior your market exhibits."

Although the keyword campaign had been in place for some time, Sellers examined two years' worth of data to analyze what actions people took after they engaged with the ads we attached to those search terms. "No matter how we tried to manipulate the campaign— budget, ad text, asset offerings, etc.—we were never able to see a real, sustained performance improvement," he said. "So, I set about finding out if we actually *should* be running the campaign, despite the topic's importance and emphasis for SAS. Maybe paid search just was not the proper platform at that time." As part of his analysis, he compared the results to the actions people took when they engaged with similar terms via an organic search. He also tracked the behavior of contacts who clicked on the ads to see what other activities they undertook to see if the campaign was beneficial in producing auxiliary actions, or those not explicitly promoted by the campaign itself. What he found was sobering: despite the high cost of the paid search campaign, only fourteen contacts opened sales opportunities with us, but none was related to the initiative being promoted. And, none of those opportunities turned into successful sales.

Armed with that kind of insight, the decision to kill the campaign was easy, but only because we had done our analytical homework and not let our emotional subjectivity or inertia get in the way of digging for the real answers about that campaign's efficacy.

Content Marketing

Content has become an especially critical component of the modern approach to marketing. Everything we do as marketers now involves some kind of content. Just offering white papers isn't enough anymore. The content used today has to be designed as "channel appropriate," meaning that the format, length, and relevancy must work in that channel. You cannot run a two-minute video in a display ad. That's why we have created an entire new family of jobs whose role is to fill in the gaps and help ensure we are offering the kind of relevant content our customers are looking for. The challenge of that content doesn't have just one form, and it is consumed differently across different channels. So we came up with a strategy for how best to procure, manage, and distribute our content across our website, blogs, social channels, campaigns, and more.

That means the people we trust for our content marketing roles have a very good understanding of all our different channels, how they function, and how they can complement each other. They use the power of analytics to assess a piece of content and understand how it fits into a marketing campaign or a customer-nurturing strategy. They also assess what kind of content works at what stage of a customer's decision journey: when do they want slides, videos, or even a book? Content marketers, therefore, are very analytically driven and act almost like consultants to a marketing campaign; they provide knowledge about what's available inside the organization and where the gaps might be.

For example, we have content creators all over our company, from leadership ranks down to data scientists who might be blogging or authoring research papers. We also hire people to provide content, like white papers. What had been happening was that without coordination and convergence, we were generating lots of duplicate content or content that was underutilized because no one knew it was there. Now, our content marketers can oversee that inventory and, by applying analytics, understand what pieces of content work best and when. For example, when we are putting together a campaign, Ericka Wilcher, a member of the digital content marketing team, works with the campaign orchestrator to perform a "content audit," in which we select content that scores best with the target customers of a particular campaign. Wilcher told me, "We are responsible for analyzing, surfacing, and recommending content that will be the best fit for a campaign."

Marketing Science

The role of the marketing data scientist or data visualization analyst is also new to marketing; this role is distinct from that of a pure data scientist. In some ways, we are still defining the different roles that fall under the umbrella of a marketing data scientist. One descriptive title I have seen for this role is "data artist" or "data storyteller." For example, Shawn Skillman is a senior marketing data visualization analyst who is skilled at modeling and storing data; he is employing the analytical tools and digging into the data we collect using a different lens. Skillman's job is to look at the data objectively to see what stories it's telling, without being tainted or biased by what someone running a campaign might want to see.

Marketing data scientists like Skillman are also able to see what happens when we make changes and tweaks; they can tell us how the story begins to change.

Another job title that currently falls under the same umbrella is what we call a "segmentation analyst." Someone running a campaign will come to a segmentation analyst like Julie Chalk, for example, and ask for her help in building a contact list that the campaign should target. To do this, Chalk relies on "scoring models," in which she parses out the key factors in a contact database that might make that person a good target for the campaign. Chalk is then able to track the results of the campaign and suggest where it might be working well or not. "We have a ton more data at our fingertips than we used to," she told me. "Part of our role is to figure out how valuable different pieces of information are and how we can make the most use of it. I didn't know jobs like this existed when I graduated college. But I love the creativity involved with it, as well as the ability to use black-and-white data to prove your hypothesis."

Chalk recalled her analysis for a campaign around one of our customer-experience software solutions. By tracking the activities of customers on our website, Chalk realized that 26 percent of visitors were dropping off before they registered for a free white paper we were offering on our product. That was great insight, because it made us question why: Were we asking too much information from the visitor? What other barriers were we putting in the way? And perhaps most importantly, what could we change to help reduce that dropout rate and create more conversions instead?

The ability of the data artists and storytellers, like Skillman and Chalk, to tackle questions like these has become a central tenet of the marketing modernization efforts we are making. They help to provide that analytical muscle that lets us make better investments in campaigns, while also letting us know when we might need to try again.

Customer Experience

Many people might think of marketing as purely an "outbound" function in which we are reaching out to potential customers. "Inbound" marketing is another evolving area in the world of marketing that ties directly to the customer decision journey, where we need to engage with customers wherever they are in their journey. We created a new position called a "customer engagement specialist" (what we used to call a "prospect development specialist"), whose role is to create deeper and more intelligent conversations with potential customers who have questions they want us to answer.

Because potential customers have so much information available to them—everything from what they obtain in a Google search to insights they get from a social media contact—it's rare that any interactions are now considered "cold." Customers have some expectations about us already, and we need to be prepared to engage them at that level. Someone might not know who we are, but he might know exactly what kind of solution he is looking for; it's up to us to understand if we can meet that need. This shift results in higher-quality interactions that have a far greater chance of conversion into actual sales than we might have experienced in the past.

While we spend much time and effort trying to land new customers, we also rely on the power of data and analytics to service our existing customers as well—something we call "relationship marketing." Once someone becomes a customer, his needs change, and it's our job to nurture that relationship and help retain his business. We have to keep up with our customers' needs and make sure they know what we can deliver to meet those needs.

One big shift we've made is to rethink the talent and skills of the people manning our customer contact center, which is itself an evolution from the traditional call center; we now address far more than

Using Chat Transcripts to Understand Customer Sentiment

Each day, the SAS customer contact center participates in hundreds of interactions with customers, prospective customers, educators, students, and the media. While the team responds to inbound calls, web forms, social media requests, and e-mails, the live-chat sessions on the corporate website make up the majority of these interactions.

The information contained in the chat transcripts can be a useful way to get feedback from customers and prospects. As a result, departments across the company frequently ask the contact center what customers are saying about the company and its products, and what types of questions they ask.

The Challenge

Chat transcripts are a source for measuring the relative happiness of those engaged with SAS. Using sentiment analysis, this information can help paint a more accurate picture of the health of customer relationships based on the content of the interactions.

The live-chat feature includes an exit survey that provides some data about visitors' overall satisfaction with the chat agent and with SAS. While 13 percent of chat visitors complete the exit survey (above the industry average), thousands of chat sessions only have the transcript as a record of participant sentiment.

Previously, analyzing chat transcripts often required the contact center to pore through the text to identify trends. With other, more pressing priorities, the manual review only provided some anecdotal information.

The Approach

Performing more formal analytics using text information is difficult due to the nature of text data. Text, unlike tabular data in databases or spreadsheets, is unstructured. There are no columns that dictate what bits of data go where. And words can be assembled in nearly infinite combinations.

For the SAS team, however, the information contained within these transcripts was a valuable asset. Using text analytics, the team could start to uncover and understand trends and connections across thousands of chat sessions.

SAS turned to SAS Text Analytics to conduct a more thorough analysis of the chat transcripts. The contact center worked with subject-matter experts across SAS to feed the text information into the analytics engine. The team used various dimensions in the analysis:

- Volume of the chat transcripts across different topics

- Web pages where the chat session originated

- Location of the customer

- Contact center agent who responded

- Duration of the chat session

- Products or initiatives mentioned within the text

In addition, North Carolina State University's Institute of Advanced Analytics began to use the chat data for a text analytics project focused on sentiment analysis. The partnership between the university and SAS helped students learn how to uncover trends in positive and negative sentiment across topics.

The Results

After applying SAS Text Analytics to the chat data, the contact center better understood the volume and type of inquiries and how they were being addressed. Often, the analysis could point to areas on the corporate website that needed updates or improvements by tracking URLs for web pages that were the launch point for a chat.

Information from chat sessions also helped fine-tune SAS's strategy. After the announcement of Windows 10, the contact center received customer questions about the operating system, including some negative sentiment about a perceived lack of support. Based on this feedback, SAS released a statement to customers assuring them that Windows 10 was an integral part of the product road map.

The project with North Carolina State University has also provided an opportunity for SAS and soon-to-be analytics professionals to continue and expand on the analysis of chat transcripts. They continue to look at the sentiment data and how it changes across different categories (products in use, duration of chat) to see if there are any further trends to explore (see figure 4-1).

Today, sentiment analysis feeds the training process for new chat agents and enables managers to highlight examples where an agent was able to turn a negative chat session into a positive resolution.

Title: Contact center workload report

What: Reports on overall inbound customer interactions by channel.

FIGURE 4-1

Contact center workload report screenshot

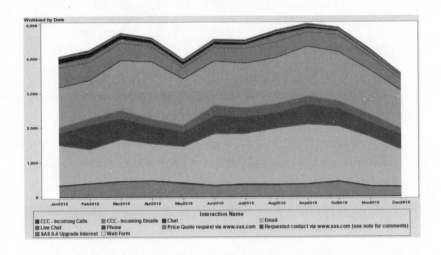

Value: Provides insight into which inbound channels are driving the most volume.

– Gives insight into how customers want to engage with us. Which channels do they use most frequently?

– Drives decisions about resource alignment to channel.

telephone calls for inbound customer interactions. When we acknowledged this, it changed how, when, and where we are available, and in what languages. "The world is so much more complex now," Chase said. "It requires a higher-level individual to help resolve customer inquiries. We need problem solvers and people committed to solving whatever issue that customer might be contacting us about."

Analytics now plays a bigger role in helping arm our customer engagement specialists with a snapshot that enables them to understand the customer, her relationship with our company, and any other relevant behavioral or historical information that can make that interaction as productive as possible for the customer. We have developed a tool called Customer 360, based on our data mart, to help in this process, but the problem is complex, especially when the timing is essential. We need to decide what information is most important for engagement specialists without drowning them in the details. We continue to evolve our systems along these lines, but the issue is so complicated that we won't ever really reach a finish line with a perfect solution, as more channels and customer data become relevant.

The new frontline of customer engagement is an emerging topic, as we've begun to recognize that marketing can play a key role in not just winning new business but retaining existing customers as well, which is another role we ask our customer engagement specialists to play.

How Do You Assess the Analytical Marketer?

When assessing candidates, there are some techniques that can help you test for an ideal analytical marketer. As you evaluate candidates' experiences, look for examples of campaigns, projects, and other key accomplishments that highlight the role that data and analytics had in decision making and evaluation. All marketers (not just the creative side) must have a "marketing analytics portfolio" that can demonstrate their use of data in the design phase, the types of analytics they employed as part of strategic decisions, the testing strategies they applied, and a performance assessment.

For example, when the directors who work for me, like Matthew Fulk or Jennifer Chase, conduct interviews, they ask candidates to

Asking the Right Questions

What sets a high-performing marketing organization apart is its ability to hire people who can find insight in data by asking the right questions. This isn't something that can be learned easily or that a lot of businesses have time for coaching and mentoring in new hires. We want candidates to tell us how they approach what they do, *but* we need to ask the right questions during the interview. We have used the STAR (situation, task, action, results) behavioral approach to formulate a list of questions to ask candidates. Some examples of behavioral questions we've used include:

- Tell me about a project you worked on where things did not go as planned? How did you respond to the challenges?

- Have you ever missed a deadline? How did this make you feel? What happened as a result?

- What is your approach to explaining a complex project or concept? Give examples.

- How do you set the right expectations with your customers?

- How do you prioritize when you have multiple projects happening at one time? Give examples.

- How do you influence decisions being made in your role?

- How do you involve others in making decisions? Give examples.

- Describe a time when you were faced with a stressful situation. How did you handle the situation?

- Give an example of a time you set a goal for yourself and achieved the goal.

share situations and projects in which they employed analytics to drive or influence a campaign. They might ask questions such as: How do you gather requirements when defining technical projects for the needs of the business user? How would a business client describe working with you? Perhaps more tellingly, if candidates progress to a third interview, they ask them to present a recent analytics project they were involved in and explain how they handled a stressful situation or overcame an error. "We want to really test if they have analytic chops and also if they can talk about it in front of a group," Chase said.

Brojan at RCI explained that his organization has also evolved its interview process along these lines; RCI relies more on panel interviews, in which it gives candidates complex business scenarios and then asks them to explain what they'd do and why.

Analytical marketers must to be able to articulate and demonstrate how they influenced change and learned from failed efforts. Marketers tend to focus on the visual and the message, which are both critical. Analytical marketers can explain the what, how, and why, or why not.

Using both verbal and written assessments to gauge a candidate's technology and "analytical IQ," in addition to their marketing savvy, is important. Request written responses to such questions as: How do you approach decision making as it relates to marketing planning and investments? What is the difference between metrics and analytics?

I look for marketers who have a clear, passionate understanding of the value of data and analytics in the work that they produce. They need to articulate value with data and analytics as an integral part of their strategies. They should justify investments backed by data and analytics. And, they must take risks, innovate, and fail, using data and analytics as their guide. When I add all this up, I am looking for marketers who have a high analytical IQ.

Evaluating Analytical IQ

After a first round of interviews, we bring finalists back for a second interview, where they are required to do a presentation. In this interview, we are specifically evaluating communication skills (how easily they can convey their material) and how they address their audience. Here's an example of what we ask of them:

Hi Candidate,

Congratulations! We would like to bring you in for a second interview. You will need to prepare for a sixty-minute meeting (thirty-minute presentation/thirty minutes for Q&A). Your audience will be the marketing sciences team and other internal customers (members of the marketing campaign teams).

Presentation details:

- Create a presentation that details a data analysis project you worked on in the past.

  - Describe the project (overall goals).

  - Describe your role and your customers.

  - Describe your tasks and how you achieved them.

  - Present the final analysis to the SAS database marketing team just as you would have to your customers.

In order to get what I want, I train and empower marketers accordingly. We have established frameworks that create governance and consistency. We have established training and certifications that are required and aligned to their objectives for performance, and we supply them with a marketing analytics portal on their desktop.

Our goal is to hire marketers who have a passion for and understand the value of data and analytics in decision making. This is not as hard as it was ten years ago. The modern marketer has evolved from being purely creative and logistics driven to appreciating data and the role of analytics. Anyone accustomed to measuring digital and social media efforts or experimenting with A/B web pages or one-to-one marketing is primed to use more advanced analytics to measure the overall value of a program. You're not killing creativity or innovation, just seeking naturally curious employees with updated skills.

Amplifying Analytical Skill Sets

The Big Data movement had a big impact on marketing at computer maker Lenovo, so much so that it helped spur an initiative to centralize its customer data and uncover new opportunities and improve the end-to-end customer experience. The Customer Insight Center of Excellence became the initiative's nerve center and arms the company's marketers with a new level of data and analysis.

As Mohammed Chaara, director of the center, told me, "We're analyzing the voice of the customer by conducting text mining on our brand mentions to help understand sentiment, identify new customer segments, and test how our messaging is resonating. And this is where all customer feedback data is getting captured. So when you layer this data on top of some of the traditional campaign measures, you get a really rich picture of your market. This has fundamentally changed how marketing operates. Now the majority of our product meetings start with customer insights, and those insights drive the actions."

Lenovo's approach represents a centralized model that provides analytics services to the marketing organization along with other business units. The Customer Insight Center of Excellence reports to R&D, and according to Chaara, this works for Lenovo "because it gives us the flexibility to draw from a broader variety of technical solutions."

In a similar way, to leverage the shared strengths of our team, we have put an internal structure in place at SAS to help team members continually learn from each other. We call these "competency centers," which are virtual task forces whose goal is to allow people inside the organization to share expertise and knowledge in five different areas: social media, analytics, marketing leadership, operations leadership, and search engine advertising.

The idea behind the competency centers is to leverage the skill sets and experience levels across the organization so that we can share best practices and learn from each other and from our mistakes. The teams, which each have fifteen members, are cross-functional; they have a representative from every marketing department and no formal management structure. Rather, they provide opportunities for team members to grow their leadership skills by helping their peers keep up with the many different changes occurring daily in the digital marketing world. We ask our people to both acquire deep expertise in an area like web search, and then share that skill with others, so that it connects with the broader view of our organizational goals.

We've already seen the centers pay off because they provide a way for team members to take risks in their daily work and then share with the broader group what they tried, why they tried it, and what happened. Everybody then reaps the benefit of that learning experience. The centers also expose people inside the organization to the capabilities of tools they might not have been aware of. The centers

The Objectives of Competency Centers

Since we focus so much on our efforts' return on investment, it's crucial that we leverage our investments in training people, which is the true value of our competency centers. At a high level, their goal is to provide integration across the organization by:

- Driving innovation.

- Improving agility.

- Developing best practices.

- Providing training and mentoring.

- Increasing communication.

How are they structured and led?

- Strong individual contributors with relevant expertise own and operate them.

- Leadership supports them as sponsors.

- The centers are cross-functional in nature and design.

- The members jointly design and drive their work.

Why are they valuable to marketing?

- The centers provide talent management and growth.

- They are a source of training and empowerment.

- They provide structure and consistency.

- They offer an opportunity for leadership.

- They build confidence and proficiency.

also support the premise that because of channel convergence, a better understanding of the channels and approaches allows for better integration and joint planning. Digital and social channels can complement or conflict with one another, so the approaches must be deliberate and planned, in addition to leveraging the organic components.

While we offer external training opportunities to team members, the competency centers are our internal training group for distributing information and expertise throughout the organization. What's so exciting about this approach is that it happens organically when someone is passionate about something and wants to share it with everyone. As a leader, I find it rewarding to see people gravitating toward areas that they are truly interested in. In this way, the competency centers serve as both forward-looking research entities, because they serve as a source for the latest experimentation, and centers for expertise that team members can rely on for answers.

For example, Skillman serves as a member of the analytics competency center. He and the other members of that team play a critical role in helping others in the organization understand the power within the data that we have collected. But rather than having people sidle up to Shawn's desk and ask him one-off questions, his role on the competency center is a way for everyone to learn from those questions when they pop up. "We are the first line of defense for anything analytically driven," he said. "And because we have a group that has a diverse background in using analytics in the organization, we have helped everyone reach a higher level of understanding of how they can use data and analytical reporting in their jobs on a daily basis."

Now that we've covered the shifts in organizational mind-set, structure, and talent, we turn now to look at what kind of leader a marketing organization needs.

How Does Your Organization Identify and Hire Analytical Marketers?

Having the right people on your team is an obvious need as you evolve into an analytical marketing organization. You might need to shift how you are hiring and who you hire. Just as importantly, you may need to take a fresh look at your training programs to modernize your existing marketing team members and leverage their experience, while also equipping them with the tools that will make their skills relevant in the analytical marketing era.

- ✓ Has your marketing organization changed the types of skill sets you want in the people you hire?

- ✓ How does your organization balance the creative side of marketing with the analytical components?

- ✓ What systems do you have in place to emphasize teamwork and collaboration among marketers above and beyond their own area of focus?

- ✓ Do you have any systems or procedures in place to help educate existing marketers and give them the analytical skills they need to compete?

- ✓ How do you enable marketers from within your organization to communicate, collaborate, and share best practices with each other?

- ✓ Are there performance objectives in place that are aligned to analytical skills?

- ✓ Are you highlighting stories of marketing's success in leveraging analytics?

5

Leading the Analytical Organization

From Responsive to Agile

Now that we've examined the big changes to organizational mindset, structure, and talent, let's look more closely at what it means to lead an analytically driven organization. What kinds of leaders does the marketing organization need? What type of leader do you have to be? How does analytics affect your interaction with your company's C-suite? We'll dig into these questions next.

Depending on the industry, marketing leaders may have come from the brand, creative, or more traditional ranks in marketing. While that is still the case for some leadership positions, marketing leaders also emerge from more technical or analytical backgrounds. It's simply not enough to do things the way we used to. Today's marketing leaders need to be technically savvy, know the value of data, and be analytically oriented. I'm not saying that the visual or brand components aren't valuable as well. That's still a big part of the job. But just having those skills is no longer enough. To lead today's modern analytical marketing organization, you need to understand how to assemble the multiple skills and disciplines inside your organization and, by playing together, create beautiful music in the form of superior engagement with your customers.

Because you now have the data and the analytics to bolster what you're pitching, it's easier to back up the stories you are telling your team and peers in other departments. Everything we are doing in marketing now is more measurable than ever, which means we can truly analyze the effectiveness of our methods. Our level of accountability is also much higher. The data, numbers, and results allow us to set, track, and hold people to objectives in a discrete and deliberate way. The insight and prediction that marketing now provides influence change and strategy.

Leading a modern marketing department also requires tenacity and the willingness to embrace constant change, because we're bombarded with a constant, daily stream of new information and emerging channels. You need to encourage your team to change with you by being honest and direct with them. Don't allow complacency; reward risk taking, and empower your team with change management support. That means encouraging them to take risks—and to fail—while also having the courage to ask what went wrong and why, so they can learn from the experience and try again.

But it's also a constant balancing act between not being complacent and not freaking out about the constant, overwhelming sense of change. A leader needs to let people know that change is OK and necessary. But it can be difficult to find a balance between pushing people too hard and giving them time to get where they need to on their own. I learned the value of understanding how each leader in an organization processes change. Everyone has a different style in communicating and consuming information. Some people talk to think; others need time to absorb, process, and then talk. Some people are energized in chaos and brainstorming; others are overwhelmed. Know your leadership team members—how they process, how they communicate, what their strengths are, and where they need a different style, especially in contrast to your own. When implementing change, be sure to overcommunicate and allow for opportunities so folks can test assumptions and share their concerns. During a recent effort in globalization, I held regular sessions called "Ask Me Anything." These were WebEx audio sessions that were offered at different times to accommodate global time zones, and my entire organization could tune in to ask anything (or submit questions in advance). I had to be honest in my answers, especially when I didn't have a good answer; it is OK for a leader to say, "I don't know yet." The entire leadership should have consistent talking points and FAQ-type documents to avoid confusion or miscommunication.

That challenge can become even more complex when you begin to push change into other countries and cultures. The Internet culture and social media use in China are very different than in the United States, for example. So how do you adapt and change to those differences instead of coming up with strategies that are standardized across the board? There's no one answer to that question, and it's something we are constantly adjusting to as we move ahead (see the discussion in chapter 3).

Leading by Example

As a modern marketing leader, you need to lead by example and use the same technology, data, and analytics tools your team members are using to tell your stories. Your job is to make them look good.

What's probably more challenging is effecting change across the entire organization, including the leadership, by defining a clear set of objectives and then utilizing the right technologies, tools, and processes to enable accountability and consistency. Some people have a system that shows the reports and gives the information, but they also have spreadsheets that don't match up. A long time ago, I told my organization, "You can keep all the spreadsheets that you want, but don't show them to me." All the data, all the analysis, all the information goes into the system of record, so that's the place where we're going to make decisions. There is a behavior shift along with the technology, the tools, and the expectations.

The other big issue we've faced, especially in the last several years, is tight budgets and limited resources. We have to be very selective with our investments. When people come with new ideas, approaches, or investments, my first questions are: Where is the data that supports your direction? How are you going to know that you've been successful? What can you show me to indicate this is the right direction? Are you willing to fail? What does that look like? When you have to be selective, you have to have metrics in place that really analyze what you can expect. The only way to answer that question is with the right data, analysis, and testing, followed by the ability to measure results and initiate change.

As an example, figure 5-1 shows a report that I look at every few weeks to understand how our different channels are performing. This report, which we call "Response by Channel," tells us the total number of responders across channels in our marketing mix. When we dig deeper into the analysis, we gain insight into how each channel is performing and get answers to the following questions:

- How is e-mail performing (clicks, conversions, opt-outs)?

- Is content syndication providing the expected value on investment?

FIGURE 5-1

Response by channel screenshot

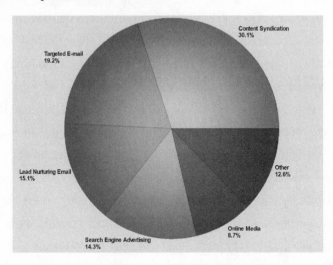

- How many impressions and conversions are we getting from online advertising and paid search?

- How many net new contacts are coming from marketing campaigns?

Because of the power of our data, we can also dive deep into any of these channels to look at performance from many different lenses. For example, if we are running a campaign on data management, we can drill down to see what channels are responding best to the campaign. We can also look at which channels are underperforming and then try to find out why.

I look at this data every two weeks or so, but it's always updated and available, which makes it even more valuable to the team members who are measuring the effectiveness of their campaigns and constantly adjusting them to boost their results. For me, this report is an example of analytical information I can use to influence our overall mix of investments and to identify areas where we might need to make changes. It's not about assessing whether something is right or wrong. Everything is fluid and always changing. Rather, I am looking at indicators in order to try different angles to drive results.

Much of my career in marketing has been directly tied to sales organizations. I learned a long time ago that sales leadership is motivated by results, metrics, and targets. So, in turn, we as a marketing organization have also embraced a marketing metrics approach.

For example, figure 5-2 shows another report we use in our conversations with the sales team that monitors the volume of leads and conversions for new sales. The report, "Lead Conversion to New Opportunities," gives the total number of leads sent to sales and how many convert to new opportunities. It also provides insight into overall lead volumes and quality and helps us answer the following questions:

- Are we tracking to our overall lead goals?

- How many leads are converting to new opportunities?

- What are the year-over-year trends?

FIGURE 5-2

Lead conversion to new opportunities screenshot

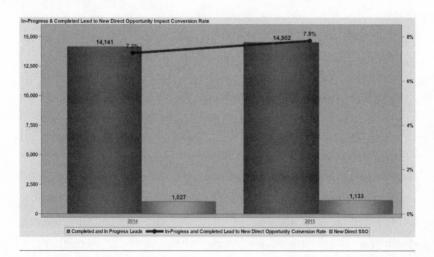

The report also exemplifies how, as a part of our organization's marketing leadership team, I use data, analytics, and metrics in marketing to have conversations, demonstrate impact, explain outcomes, justify investments, and gain credibility with my colleagues on the executive team. And, not just with sales, but with finance, IT, and many other constituents. My use of analytics in marketing is both deliberate and necessary. I need first to demonstrate my expectations for marketers when being analytical. Effectively using data, analytics, and the corresponding tools is core to my leadership role. Consistently utilizing the systems, applications, and reports is part of a communication strategy, and it serves us well in building business cases as well as continually demonstrating value.

Our financial approach is centered on forecasting and regular budget management, but a few times each year, I meet with the CEO and the CMO to review large-scale investments like advertising or events. Advertising discussions have changed over the years, increasingly shifting to digital investments and a broader set of offerings. In order to gain approval for continual growth in these investments, I have to demonstrate value.

Historically, it's been difficult to measure the direct impact of marketing on revenue. But by putting analytics into the picture, I'm injecting fact-based decision making into what used to be purely a creative process. That gives more accountability to those results and more certainty about how to mitigate risk and manage costs.

The real power is in tapping into those insights through reports like our "Pipeline and Revenue Impact by Sales Business Unit" (see figure 5-3). From this report, we can see the percentage of the overall sales pipeline and revenue affected by our marketing campaigns across all sales business units, with the dotted line as our target. The percentages show to what degree marketing touched a prospect or a final sale with our campaigns, thus providing a real connection

FIGURE 5-3

Pipeline and revenue impact by sales business unit screenshot

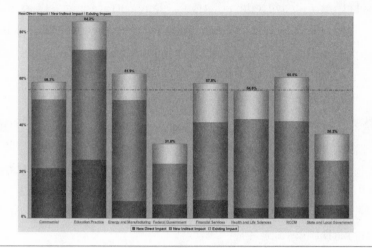

between our efforts and the bottom line for the organization. They also help us answer the following questions:

- Are we tracking to our overall pipeline and revenue impact goals?

- What's our overall return-on-marketing investment?

I use this tool to talk about the overall pipeline, where gaps might be, and where we can shift investments to best support sales. Marketing has traditionally been seen as a cost center, so in that view, analytics and reports like these help ensure that you're not overspending in the wrong places and enable you to make informed changes along the way. In a more current view, marketing is seen as a potent driver of profitable growth, even as the customer's digital footprint becomes more complex.

Consider how much business is conducted in the digital realm, where just about everything generates data streams. In today's world, marketers are in the best position to capture customer insights from those data streams with analytics. Those insights will have an impact on the role that marketing plays as both an owner of the customer relationship and a steward of the customer experience.

Analytics has always been a part of marketing in particular industries. CMOs need to show value and revenue impact, and can't demonstrate either without some level of analytics, preferably a sophisticated

How to Demonstrate Value

My approach to demonstrating value as a marketing leader is twofold:

1. Measuring the specific outcomes across

    -   Exposure

    -   Reach

    -   Pipeline and revenue impact

2. Demonstrating the use of data and analytics in decision making through

    -   Targeting and segmentation

    -   Optimization

    -   Predictive analytics

When I meet with my CEO and CMO, I spend a lot of time showing them outcomes: how our pipeline has grown, for instance, or how many leads we have turned over to sales. But I also explain how I am using analytics in my own decision making to help improve those outcomes. I balance the amount of time I talk about outcomes with my rationale for what I'm doing to improve them. It can't be too much of one or the other, if I really want to get leadership behind my plan.

one. Today it's not about a single department or a single person or a group doing analytics; it's about changing the entire culture in marketing. If you want to encourage critical thinkers and problem solvers, you have to change their mind-set and show them that analytics will deliver higher value and help them be more competent and more accountable. But that has to change across the organization.

Telling Your Story

Sometimes our team needs to engage in shameless self-promotion. We need to tell stories about the interesting things and projects the team is involved in to ensure that the rest of the organization understands our value. We have to deliberately build credibility for marketing. My job as a marketing head is to ensure that sales, IT, finance, and other departments know the value we are delivering by communicating early and often about the efforts that are affecting our shared success.

Brenda Hodge, a marketing executive with a leading health-care innovation company, agrees that we need to be responsible for building our own credibility with other leaders and departments, and that's something we can do through storytelling. She said, "You can share the big-picture numbers, but then you need to bring it down to the level where you are giving them examples of deals that you closed and the activities those prospects engaged in before they became customers or renewed their contract. You have to make the data come to life. When you can connect the dots for people and share those stories, you'll start to see light bulbs going off."

We also engage in some joint storytelling with other department heads we are collaborating with to drive new sales and deeper relationships with our customers. For example, my counterpart in IT and I share the story of how we are working together to help drive bottom-line results through our partnership in providing the data and tools that are landing new deals. We objectively show that the investments we have made in a certain technology are empowering us to a particular result in our sales pipeline. Both departments show that we are more than just cost centers and are absolutely critical to the success of the organization. With the help of the data, we demonstrate our impact.

One way I know for sure that this approach has value is when leaders use what I gave them to tell their own stories. If you can get your CMO or CEO to tell the data and analytics marketing story for you, then you know it was highly valued.

Setting Objectives

You can only change behavior when you change someone's objectives, and then make it very clear that you are going to measure that person against those objectives. Of course, we have always had performance metrics. But in order to track our own performance objectives as a marketing organization, we have established a set of reports we can monitor daily via a dashboard. We can look at how team members are progressing toward their individual performance objectives, and then the channels, campaigns, and departments to see how we are tracking against our goals at each tier. Figure 5-4 shows an example of the global-level goals and metrics that we track.

The key is to ensure that individuals don't chase their own goals at the expense of our goals as an organization. We want team members to care deeply about their channel or area of specialty, but we also want them to care about the rest of the business as well. That's why our managers work with people to use the internal human resource management system, setting performance objectives whose outcomes trickle through the organization.

We continue tracking our targets and seeing what levers to pull and adjustments to make to hit the targets over time. We've learned to

FIGURE 5-4

Sample goals and metrics

Goals	Sample metrics
Increase the value and relevance of the brand	• Reach and impressions • Sentiment analysis • Channel and content performance
Positive imapact on pipeline build and revenue	• Percent impact on pipeline • Impact on revenue • Demand generation—volume, quality, conversion, etc.
Engage, service, and grow the community	• Customer satisfaction levels • Response levels • Net promoter score

be careful about setting what you might call "hard" targets, because so many factors can affect them. We also think about different indicators in different ways. I might not care about our click-through rates on an ad, for instance, as much as I care about how many sales conversions we ended up with. But if the click-through rate drops, I may need to investigate what caused that change. You need to be constantly evolving and learning as you monitor your results. That's what will help you keep things fresh and give you reason to look for things you may not have noticed before.

Moving Forward as an Analytical Leader

Another key aspect of "leading by example" is your approach in inspiring others. Your approach to continual change as you embrace the principles of becoming an analytical marketing organization is especially challenging. Change can be threatening to some, and a different level of engagement is needed to be part of a continually changing environment. My leadership approach to inspiring agents of change is actually pretty simple. I believe leaders should be genuine and authentic in order to build the kinds of relationships to effectively run a modern marketing organization. That includes adopting such best practices as:

- Be truthful and transparent; establish honest, open communication all the time.

- Engage constantly; this is *our* journey.

- Be willing to eliminate barriers.

- Be decisive; keep things moving.

Table 5-1 provides a few descriptions you might find useful in rethinking your role as a marketing leader, innovator, and influencer.

Cameron Dow, the vice president of marketing at SAS who oversees Canada and Latin America, noted that you also can't underestimate the importance of building a case for why you're asking people to change. "It can be easy to feel like you have done all the analysis and have come up with the right thing to do," he said,

TABLE 5-1

Rethinking your role as a marketing leader, innovator, influencer

Leader	Innovator	Influencer
Be the evangelist.	Be the spark.	Be the storyteller.
Authentic, transparent	Passionate, confident	Inquisitive, engaging
Provide clarity and vision.	Take risks, reward failure.	Advocate the vision.
Decisive	Illustrative	Collaborative

"while at the same time, you haven't walked anyone else through your thought process, so you end up failing to bring anyone else along with you on your journey. That's why it's critical to keep your team and your stakeholders involved in any transformation effort all along that journey."

One approach we have found effective is to form a guiding coalition within our organization made up of people who understand why change is needed and agree on where everyone is headed, together. We work with this group to create a vision of where we want to go and then rely on them to help us communicate the path forward until the changes become part of our organizational culture. It's not something that happens as a onetime event, though. We still spend a significant amount of time designing and communicating our vision, as we continue to adjust to the changes that are always happening. The key is to make it clear to people why changes are being made.

As you take your organizations through this journey, there will be casualties. Some will choose not to engage and prefer a different path or environment. Some will take on stronger leadership roles and become trusted advisers. The beauty of the analytical journey is how many directions we can take and how much opportunity we have constantly available to us. I have witnessed wonderful discovery, amazing growth, and a renewed confidence across the organization. That's the power of culture at work.

Prepare for Surprises along the Way

As part of our analytical marketing organization, I have tried to lead with the right balance of collaboration and decision making. I've pushed to move ideas, concepts, and change forward, while also making sure to stop and calibrate along the way. Efforts can get stuck, spinning too much in what cannot be accomplished or bogged down in process or people. As leaders, we have to move obstacles, redirect, or reimagine. Empowering others in this process is critical, giving them permission to drive to a decision or, when necessary, making the decisions.

My favorite part of this entire process is to watch an idea come to life. It often catches me by surprise, mostly because those closest to it don't always see their success or value. I often have to remind others to share their stories, send examples, and promote their discoveries. Then, it is my job to evangelize their results, all the way to the top.

Give People Permission to Fail

Data, technology, advanced analytics, methodology, and a strong analytical culture drive innovation. Having data and analysis at your disposal encourages people to be inquisitive and challenge the status quo, and not be afraid of trying. Permission to fail is a key aspect to inspiring innovative ideas. Individuals need rewards for taking risks and bringing innovations forward. At the simplest level, innovation is about problem solving, testing, and adjusting efforts. Innovation resonates for marketers in the approach to new channels and communication methods. Innovative marketers will leverage analytics to take more calculated risks and, most importantly, have the confidence to be agile in responding to the market. If they are empowered with the tools, the permission, and the creativity, they will be strong leaders and better marketers.

The impact of marketing analytics results in a more intelligent marketer and a better customer experience. We can be smarter, but we also have to be more agile. Becoming more agile presumes a lot of things—a higher level of response, more flexibility, and anticipating needs, not just reacting. Agile marketing or proactive marketing is the goal.

But, first, you need to understand how agile or proactive the marketing organization is. Then, define what being agile means to your business. The next step is to assess the drivers that make you more or less agile—process, technology, and people.

Once an assessment of agility is understood, you can prioritize what to change. Identify barriers, determine intersection points with analytics needs, and define cultural impacts. There are, of course, risks associated with being agile. Humans make mistakes, and there need to be safeguards in place. But there also needs to be a culture that rewards failure and allows people to fail fast. As a basic tenant of innovation, failure must be seen as progress.

Marketing agility is also about choosing the right "attitude." Agility needs to be ingrained in the culture as an expectation, not an exception. A sense of urgency and a level of accountability that align to a clear set of objectives drive behavior, just like all other aspects of the business. Some people cannot be effective in that mode, so it is imperative that they know up front and either adapt or move out.

When Felicia Ramsey, a marketing manager at SAS, started her career in media and advertising, she said that the only way anyone could measure the potential effectiveness of a campaign was to conduct a focus group, especially since it was so hard to assess the impact of a print or TV campaign. Making adjustments on the fly became difficult; you had to wait until the completion of the campaign to see the results.

With digital advertising, that's all changed. "We don't waste our time on anything we can't measure our ROI anymore," Ramsey explained. "That allows us to do more of things that work while doing less of things that don't work." With digital tools, we as marketers can also experiment and try new things without making the kinds of investments we once needed to. "We have built a culture that encourages and rewards us for taking risks and trying something different," Ramsey said. "I've worked in other places where doing that might be held against you. Here you can be creative and comfortable about experimenting."

A key lesson we've learned is to give marketers the freedom to test and learn so they can make intelligent decisions that will drive change. Since we began applying marketing optimization techniques, our conversion rates on outbound marketing campaigns have tripled, while associated communication costs are dropping. There has been a reduction in list size of 14 percent, a reduction in e-mail opt-outs of 20 percent, and an increase in click-through rates of 25 percent—all of which translates into higher-quality leads, reduced costs, and an improved customer or prospect experience. Achieving that kind of optimization has a direct impact on results, and it indirectly increases marketers' confidence level. There is far less guesswork and much more time and energy invested in strategies to connect with customers.

A great example of how, by using data and analytics, we are able to be more agile and experiment with new techniques is the evolution of our website, www.sas.com. With millions of visitors to our site, most of whom initially find us through an organic web search, analytics is critical for determining how we leverage a person's time on the site. With scoring and nurturing efforts, we have experienced conversion rates at 20 percent to 30 percent. Just as importantly, we have enhanced the overall experience for our customers when they do visit our website by making ourselves available to talk with them if they have questions. That's something we've added with our relatively new, integrated, online chat capabilities that allow members of our customer contact center to respond in real time to visitors' questions.

Adding the chat technology actually began as a skunk-works test program under Aaron Hill, Senior Director of Digital Strategy and

Marketing Analytics at Work

Using Data to Justify Additional Resources

In the last decade, live chat has gone from a website curiosity to a mainstay on corporate sites. For companies selling business-to-business solutions, the use of chat is an immediate way to answer questions and establish dialogues with customers, even on their first visit.

SAS began investing significantly in chat resources in 2008, and each passing month brought new levels of engagement. Initially, the contact center operated from 8:30 a.m. to 5 p.m. eastern (US), Monday through Friday. The staff answered questions, provided links to resources, and often initiated a valuable early sales contact with prospective customers.

By 2013, the team realized that web traffic supported the need for coverage later in the day to help meet the requirements of customers in the western United States and Canada. As a temporary measure, the team started to work an altered shift from 12 p.m. to 8 p.m. as a pilot, but that left the group understaffed earlier in the day.

At the same time, the scope of the group supporting live chat expanded to include social media engagement on Twitter, LinkedIn, and other channels. Soon, the contact center was at a crossroads. With a longer workday, more engagement options, and the same staff, marketing leadership had to make changes to meet the increased demand.

The Challenge

The contact center team faced a dilemma found in many marketing groups. The team supported a high-volume activity, but there weren't enough resources to cover additional efforts such as more channels (social media plus live chat) and a longer workday.

Because the contact center worked closely with inside sales to pass on leads, the marketing leaders proposed a partnership with their sales counterparts. Marketing would increase the operating hours for the contact center to include more coverage for West Coast customers and others on our website later in the day. It would also expand its reach to include more complete coverage of social media channels, as well as discussion forums, as part of a global social media monitoring and response program.

To justify the increased resources, the contact center turned to historical data on chat traffic to determine:

- Web visitors whose behavior indicated a likely lead

- Chat acceptance rate

- Rate of chats to leads

- Number of leads passed to sales

- Rate of chats to sales conversions

- Close rate of deals originated by chat

The Approach

The marketing leadership team used the data from contact center interactions to justify hiring additional resources. The team applied SAS algorithms to historical live-chat results, creating a virtual view of the results the sales team could expect with additional resources.

The team applied the same approach to lead conversions and close rates and also added resources to the analysis. Based on these extrapolations, the marketing team could predict the workload and sales leads from each additional staff member, and what that would mean to the bottom line. The analysis also showed how the team could interact more effectively across social channels and, as an additional benefit, help SAS recruit attendees to events.

With better data about the historical performance of live-chat sessions, the team members accurately predicted the outcomes of adding additional resources. Rather than simply asking for resources based on gut feel, they made a strong, data-driven presentation to executive leadership. They got the approval, and the contact center hired new staff.

The Results

Soon after adding the new resources, the team began to see that the expanded contact center was living up to expectations. Extended coverage hours and additional contact center resources helped generate more leads for sales from inbound channels. The data showed that these leads had the highest likelihood of converting to sales opportunities and revenue. The additions contributed directly to the bottom line and validated the analysis conducted to justify the new positions.

The team has also become more active in social channels, expanding the company's presence and allowing the marketing organization to be more proactive. For example, a new Twitter handle—@SAS_Cares—gives customers an additional service channel for quick responses to their questions as well as timely notifications and helpful tips.

Technology, who recognized that all the content on our website might actually be confusing to a visitor, especially someone who simply wanted a price quote. Hill told me he equated the situation with entering a home improvement store and wandering the aisles looking for the right product. How happy we become, therefore, when someone steps out from behind the cash register to help us. In the end, we as customers appreciate help and buy more as a result. Hill thought chat could bring similar benefits to our customers and business. He was right; we've seen a much higher conversion rate among visitors to our website who engage with us via chat.

Similarly, we continue to experiment with other aspects of interacting with customers through the website, such as how much information we require someone to give before, say, downloading a white paper. While we might think we need twelve items of information about a person and her company, for example, we might see a high rate of opt-outs when we've made the barrier too high. By using the data as our guide to understanding that behavior, perhaps we really only need to ask for six critical pieces of information, which will in turn boost the number of people who download our white paper. "It's all about using the data to help us understand how to make the experience for our customers better," Hill said.

None of this would happen if our marketers weren't comfortable testing, measuring, changing, and justifying marketing activities. We let analytics decide the best approach and reward the effort.

There is a saturation point, so, as leaders, we need to pay attention to warning signs of the flawed aspects of being agile. We also need to watch the level of risk, the number of failures, and the volume of changing expectations. If we don't, it can lead to the wrong behavior and negative outcomes. Finding the balance is key, and ensuring that data and analytics are components of the approach to being agile increases our success rate.

Leadership Advice

As someone who has evolved as a leader and learned some lessons along the way, I offer the following advice for those who aspire to lead their own analytical marketing organization:

- Be willing to rock the boat.

- Be willing to be wrong.

- Be willing to be right.

- Be willing to compromise.

- Be authentic.

- Be confident.

- Be deliberate.

- Trust, deliver, respect.

Make It Personal

As leaders, we often believe that our success is defined and validated by the level of innovation (or idea generation) we have achieved or the amount of knowledge gained. Or, even more dangerously, when we seek perfection. As you embark on transformational experiences, it is important to leverage your guiding coalition to execute effectively. Make it happen; don't just talk about it. Use the process and experiences as constant learning opportunities, being willing to accept that knowledge is only powerful if it is enriched. And, getting it *done* is better than a constant push for perfection.

There is a lot of advice available for all of us as leaders—plenty of training, books, tests, and coaching to guide us along the way. None of that really replaces the value of just having experience—time to learn, make mistakes, and change. Part of leading in a transformation is about having confidence in your decisions. Confidence can take on different forms. My style is to be very open and engaged, both in work and in my personal life. I act and react very honestly, and I am not fearful of being wrong or not knowing the answer. I rely on my guiding coalition; together we can fill the gaps. I am not in this alone. Take the example of Amy Cuddy, who gave a popular TED Talk about body language.[1] I heard her speak at a conference in Las Vegas in October 2015, where she said that "real confidence comes across as honest and open, not as arrogance."[2] She was referring to your body language when you are telling your story. If you are authentically honest and open, and believe your story, it comes across fluidly.

As a leader, my last piece of advice is to take the time to know your own personal story. Write it down. Be introspective about your style, your values, your principles, and what motivates you. Who are you and what were your influences?

Did you know that you can drop off dirty laundry at a Laundromat and someone will wash and fold it for you? Well, it was true in 1979, when I was fifteen years old and got my first job at a Laundromat. I have been working ever since. Most of my jobs were in retail, but I also worked at a check-processing center, as a babysitter, and—the job that everyone should have at least once—as a waitress (or waiter). Work is fulfilling, and regardless of the job, I am always driven to excel. It might be pride or work ethic. But I think it is probably a huge sense of accountability. I like that others can depend on me and trust me to get the job done. That characteristic was instilled in me from a young age, and I saw my parents demonstrate that same commitment and diligence. They both worked hard to provide for our family and to enjoy life. My mother came to the United States from Cuba in her twenties and started a whole new life. That takes confidence and stamina. My father joined the navy at eighteen and eventually reached senior management at IBM. That takes courage and determination. They were both loving and supportive, and they had high expectations of us throughout our lives. I know how fortunate I am.

Confidence, stamina, strong work ethic, accountability, and kindness were all my influences. All my life, I have been surrounded by love and support, which make me who I am. They make me a better person and ground me and make me authentic—I hope.

A life story has its ups and downs—tragic moments that last a lifetime but, over time, become more part of you than a moment in time. When I was thirteen, my aunt was dying of cancer, and in 1977, there wasn't much anyone could do for her. My maternal grandfather was in his sixties and had come to this country in the mid-1960s from Cuba and had to start life over again. He had actually immigrated from Lebanon to Cuba, so during his life, he had seen his share of chaos and hardship. He couldn't bear to lose his eldest daughter, so hours before her death, he took his own life. My first experience with death was burying both my aunt and my grandfather. The images of that time are vivid in my memory. He will always be one of the most influential people in my life. He was so incredibly patient and loving. Even without knowing the English language, he found a way to work, and he worked so hard. He was eager to learn English, so I can remember hours sitting with him telling him the words in English and him teaching me Spanish. He showed me what it means to experience and sacrifice. He also taught me that a little salt on an orange is the only way to eat it. It was my *abuelo* who made me a kind and compassionate person.

On March 17, 1987, my father died at the age of fifty-three. I was twenty-two years old and terrified. As you would expect, at first there was shock and numbness that don't have a real description. I had to do some pretty fast growing up at this point. My mother was unprepared for life without him. In the days leading up to my father's bypass surgery, he had prepared to die. He provided me with very explicit instructions about moving money and other documents, should he not survive the surgery. When the time came, I had to follow the instructions. It has been twenty-six years, and my dad missed so much of my life. There is truth in feeling his presence. That day changed me forever, and I continue to learn from him. It was his strength, confidence, and compassion as a person that have also changed the course of my life. My dad gave me self-assurance and a sense of curiosity. To this day, my mom is still teaching me about patience and courage.

In finding my authentic self as a leader, my most influential life moments have been welcoming my children into this world. I know that may be expected, but it is no less important to the story. Understanding the meaning and feeling of unconditional love for someone will shape your heart. Leading as much with your heart as your head is a valuable trait that I cherish. I also believe that passion comes from those experiences that touch your heart. My children are constantly teaching me how to be passionate about life.

. There are certainly more chapters in my story. If you take the time to write down your own story, it becomes clear how those experiences influenced you as a leader. Your story gives you a perspective on your own strengths and weaknesses. Your story will define your authenticity as a person. When you write down your story, it becomes clear how it influences you as a leader and how you can leverage your strengths—and weaknesses—to become more effective at leading an analytical marketing organization.

Have You Changed Your Approach to Leading an Analytical Marketing Organization?

As your marketing organization shifts to analytical marketing, you'll need to change how you think about leading your team and how you interact with your peers in other departments and even the executives in the C-suite. Consider how you might need to shift your current approach to your team members and how you sell the value of your department to the company's bottom line. Ask questions such as:

- ✓ What does your marketing dashboard look like and who pays attention to it?

- ✓ If you want to understand the impact of a campaign or program, is that information readily available to you—on your desktop or mobile device?

- ✓ If you want data or analysis to support your investment decisions, how easily can you access the information?

- ✓ Do your marketers regularly come to you with insights or stories about your customers and the marketing efforts? Are they in active advisory roles?

- ✓ Would having access to new analytical reports change how marketing interacts with executive-level leadership?

- ✓ Has understanding how marketing delivers value and impact on revenue for the company shifted?

✓ Have you gotten executive leaders' support for adding the digital or analytics talent and resources required to make the shift to an analytical marketing organization?

✓ What can you as a leader do to help ensure your marketing organization continues to be dynamic and embraces future changes?

CONCLUSION

What's Next—Your Call to Action

In the preceding chapters, I have outlined the path that we at SAS have taken to transform ourselves into an analytical marketing organization. Along the way, I have shared some insights from other organizations and some tips for how you might begin your own transformation. But I don't think there is only one way to do that: each organization has its own baseline and opportunities to chase and challenges to surmount.

To me, the kind of analytical marketing culture you're trying to build should have the following characteristics:

- Engagement

- Collaboration

- Focus

- Courage

But I'm also a pragmatist. I don't think there is ever a true destination or end to this evolution. At SAS, we continue to explore how to keep up with the expectations and needs of our customers. There's no doubt that new tools will emerge, and new data sources will be tapped into. You can learn from how we have rethought our organization and structure to best take advantage of inevitable changes in the future.

I wish there had been a how-to guide available to us when we started searching for answers at beginning of our journey. I have given you practical ways, at the end of each chapter, to conduct some self-evaluation and provided tips for starting change in your organization. The "Sample Job Descriptions" in the next chapter, would have been invaluable to us several years ago, because they literally didn't exist at the time: we had to construct them from scratch. They can serve as a shortcut on your journey.

As a businessperson, I know that I want advice that I can use *tomorrow*. With that in mind, here are my thoughts on the three things you can start to do tomorrow (or Monday morning) to begin your transformation into an analytical marketing organization:

1. *Evaluate—know where you stand*

   - What is your analytical culture? Begin by finding out what tools you have available and how you use analytics to make decisions.

   - Find the data and own it. Ditch your spreadsheets.

   - Understand your customer. Quickly evangelize and operationalize. Use data and analytics to tell your customer experience story. Share the story across levels, departments, and intersection points.

2. *Nurture relationships—build a guiding coalition of change agents*

   - Fully integrate a communication strategy throughout your internal organization and the company. Let people, including in the C-suite, know what you want to do, when you want to do it, and why you're doing it.

   - Jointly design and implement—with balance and intent. This journey isn't just for the marketing department: you need partners. Talk with your peers in other departments and find ways to team up and drive results together.

   - Relationships matter inside your organization and outside it.

3. *Embrace change—drive action and celebrate wins*

   - Establish milestones, objectives, and outcomes. Don't let projects spin; it is easy to want perfection, but you never will reach it. If you can't measure your progress, you'll be unable to show the ROI from your investments or keep people excited about the journey you're asking them to take.

   - Challenge the obvious. What insights can you gain by looking into those dark corners that others have overlooked?

   - Provide a platform to expose for your efforts; partake in some shameless self-promotion.

SAMPLE JOB DESCRIPTIONS

Data Visualization Analyst

Summary

Designs new approaches to analytics for strategic use across the business. Builds reports and analytics that provide key business insights used for data-driven decision making. Possesses a strong business acumen coupled with demonstrated technical ability to know how to develop, explore, analyze, and present data and solutions to a business audience.

Primary Responsibilities

- Takes a proactive, consultative approach to analytics. Asks the right questions of the data and makes proactive recommendations aligned to overall business strategy.

- Provides project leadership on marketing analytics requests, including requirements management, report development, testing, and communications to stakeholders, and so on.

- Performs data analysis from multiple data sources and builds reports for projects such as executive dashboards, nurturing, customer journey analytics, lead performance analysis, digital and social campaign analytics, customer response analysis, return on marketing investment analysis, attribution, and so on.

- Communicates and presents analysis and insights to internal customers and executive management.

- Contributes to the efforts of building and maintaining a comprehensive reporting and tracking strategy for optimal marketing campaign performance.

- Evaluates business needs and improves efficiencies and capabilities through the use of technology. This includes automation and improvement to operational processes aligned to the strategy of improving overall analytics.

- Connects cross-divisional analytics and data initiatives.

- May train personnel in scope and functionality of processes, systems, and solutions.

- Performs other duties as assigned.

Segmentation Analyst

Summary

Provides consultation on various campaign design and implementation strategies, including segmentation, e-mail marketing best practices, industry research, campaign logic, data source review, marketing campaign analysis and evaluation, and so on.

Primary Responsibilities

- Leads overall strategy and applies best practices for segmentation and e-mail. This includes targeting, frequency, order, and timing on all inbound and outbound e-mail communications.

- Develops and implements segmentation logic that sends the right communication, at the right time, based on customer behavior, actions, and journey stage.

- Proactively questions and searches for insights on customer behavior aligned to customer journey marketing campaigns. Presents data-driven recommendations and strategies to team members and management based on findings.

- Analyzes marketing campaign data and evaluates overall performance of channels, assets, conversions, leads, pipeline, and revenue impact. Presents data-driven recommendations and strategies to team members and management based on findings.

- Provides feedback to enhance data available in internal CRM system.

- Contributes to the efforts of building and maintaining a comprehensive campaign reporting and tracking strategy.

- Provides superior customer service to our internal clients and external suppliers.

- May train personnel in scope and functionality of processes, systems, and solutions.

- Performs other duties as assigned.

Content Marketing Specialist

Summary

Content marketing is the practice of creating, curating, and distributing relevant and compelling content in a consistent fashion to a targeted buyer, focusing on all stages of the buying process, from brand awareness through to brand evangelism. Content marketing must include strategic planning, content creation, distribution, and metrics for multiple stages of the buying cycle to multiple customer personas, through different channels. Buyers want to be informed, educated, and entertained about topics they are interested in. The content marketing specialist works closely with subject-matter experts, channel experts, editors, writers, partners, and external resources to plan, evaluate, and commission new content ideas and solicit and share insights to empower campaign teams with high-performing content. The resulting offers should drive reach, engagement, sentiment, conversion, education, and commitment from target buyers and customers.

Primary Responsibilities

- Leads and manages a campaign-focused content strategy that supports business objectives and is crafted to deliver a high-quality prospect and customer experience, honing methods that work for the brand or product.

- Drives content story arc or narrative development for each initiative campaign, as well as across all initiatives based on sanctioned messaging.

- Actively seeks knowledge in topic trends, developments, and terminology to get an outside-in view.

- Understands the structure of a good story and how it plays out in different media.

- Maintains an ongoing inventory or audit of content relevant to key initiatives and conducts periodic competitive audits.

- Evaluates existing assets according to agreed-upon content criteria to propose whether they need to be retired, repurposed, or revamped for continued use.

- Builds gap analysis and content plan for creation or commissioning of new content to fill gaps along the customer journey.

- Recommends cornerstone assets to be used along each phase of the customer journey.

- Integrates content plan with blog, video, advertising, search, social, content syndication, third-party community and sponsorship, and e-commerce strategies, and so on.

- Owns cross-initiative, high-level content development programs and manages these in collaboration with larger initiative content plans.

- Governs or approves the creation or purchase of new campaign content in alignment with the collective content plan for the initiative.

- Collaborates on the development of editorial content calendars.

- Reviews new campaign content for consistency in terms of style, quality, visuals, and tone of voice, and that it is optimized for search and user experience for all channels including web, advertising, social media, e-mail, and video.

- Curates content to develop new assets from existing (infographics, ebooks, blogs, etc.) using internal resources or third-party creative vendors.

- Researches and recommends new and innovative types of content to develop, mapped to appropriate channels.

- Determines what to measure and then analyzes content and program performance.

- Holds regular meetings and directional check-ins with sister organizations and global counterparts.

- Interfaces with "content factories," internally and externally, to procure.

- Explores and recommends content management system tool.

- Influences processes to ensure content development is completed in a manner that optimizes both efficiency and quality.

- Implements best practices for content creation, reuse, and optimization.

Digital Marketing Specialist Job Family

Summary

Responsible for planning, coordinating, and executing digital strategy. Role will include managing and executing a wide variety of digital projects (web, search, e-mail, campaigns, etc.), delivering strategic guidance to clients; collaborating with many departments across the company to help them leverage the digital channel to meet company goals.

Digital Marketing Specialist's Primary Responsibilities

- Ensures that the digital channel meets the needs of the intended audience and is presented most effectively, adhering to integrity of content and company standards, best practices, and industry regulations.

- Builds client relationships by understanding the client's business objectives and delivering digital guidance and expertise based on an understanding of user behavior, to align with corporate goals and initiatives.

- Delivers digital services ranging from consultative to full administrative support by creating web pages, providing prototypes, wireframes, templates, and so on.

- Incorporates analyzed metrics and usability trends to validate current strategy and effectively make recommendations for improvements.

- Participates on cross-functional teams with the goal of ensuring consistency, accuracy, quality, and globalization of sales and marketing activities or deliverables across major geographies.

- Identifies changes in digital marketing and recommends appropriate strategies that will ultimately maximize company profit. Stays abreast of related industry trends and technologies by doing online research, evaluating other third-party websites, and attending professional conferences.

Search Analyst's Primary Responsibilities

- Is responsible for driving and executing on search strategy to protect and grow search for the company, in support of business goals.

- Works with internal teams to enhance findability of company content.

- Provides SEO analysis and recommendations in coordination with elements and structure of websites and web pages.

- Provides recommendations and executes strategies across teams for content development in coordination with search goals—general and keyword specific.

- Performs keyword research to optimize findability for existing content and uncover new opportunities.

- Drives strategy and execution on paid search campaigns.

- Evaluates search results and performance across channels and communicates via reporting and presentations to stakeholders.

- Uses search specific tools such as BrightEdge and Marin as well as other web tools such as Adobe Experience Manager, Google Analytics, and SAS Customer Experience Analytics.

- Keeps pace with SEO, search engine, social media, and Internet marketing industry trends and developments.

- Acts as centralized program management for search globally.

Web Production Specialist's Primary Responsibilities

- Manages, posts, and edits content for all digital properties, including websites, portals, e-mails and e-mail newsletters, and other online communications media.

- Assists with managing content updates and functionality upgrades, which support activities including but not limited to marketing projects and campaigns, internal communications, and corporate website updates and upgrades.

- Works with internal teams to develop and improve websites.

- Follows existing marketing and communication strategies.

- Handles routine requests on OSS-supported web properties or channels such as creation of web products based on templates.

- Gathers requirements for each request and executes using templates.

- Maintains integrity of existing web properties.

- Performs regular reviews of the website to ensure consistency and working links. Handles or escalate issues as appropriate.

- Monitors web usage for digital assets and provides reports for management review.

- Performs user acceptance testing for accessibility and functionality as required.

- Provides on-call/after-hours support.

- Consults with appropriate staff to develop, organize, and update content as well as recommend and develop enhancements and modifications to content.

- Works closely with the team to improve site functionality and develop new capability and features.

- Troubleshoots issues as they arise and determines best solution.

- Trains new users on different website platforms, as needed.

- Keeps pace with web industry trends and developments.

Web Usability Specialist's Primary Responsibilities

- Performs usability testing and analysis.

- Acts as the subject-matter expert on user-testing techniques and technology.

- Requires an understanding of voice-of-consumer methodologies including heuristic evaluation, contextual inquiry, tree analysis, card sorting, gap analysis, and competitive benchmarking.

- Able to apply human factors principles to the digital channel.

Web Governance Specialist's Primary Responsibilities

- Understands website governance and auditing methodologies.

- Develops and maintains standards documentation.

- Able to identify accessibility opportunities and propose implementation plans.

- Collaborates with teams to support global content rollouts.

- Manages the web governance program or software to administer accounts, create and analyze reports, assist in correcting identified errors, and disseminating status of updates and reports.

Digital Analytics Specialist's Primary Responsibilities

- Educates and empowers business partners to leverage digital web analytics as business drives for fact-based decision making.

- Configures and uses web analytics data to recognize patterns and trends and make client-facing recommendations with a view to increasing traffic, conversions, and ultimately revenue.

- Implements tracking codes and systems or IT configurations as needed for web-tracking capabilities.

- Creates scalable, innovative approaches to extracting, managing, and analyzing customer data.

- Collaborates with various internal teams to create and generate reports.

- Implements and evaluates A/B testing.

- Provides regular reports about performance, trends, and opportunities for web user experience and related digital activities.

- Provides web data analysis identifying user patterns, trends, behaviors, and opportunities for improvement.

Digital Information Architect's Primary Responsibilities

- Provides positive user experience by planning and designing the information structure for websites and web applications.

- Creates wireframes that illustrate site layout, navigation, controls, and content prioritization.

- Develops and maintains site map and wireframe mockups, usage scenarios, prototypes, specifications, and other design documents to communicate design ideas.

- Creates navigational models that are aligned with the defined user experience and business requirements.

- Works with development teams to make sure that the information architecture reflects the customer's needs.

- Collaborates with designers on visual comps and provides input from an information architecture perspective.

- Collaborates with writers, developers, and fellow designers to take a project from initial idea to final output.

- Contributes to usability test planning and contributes to user-experience satisfaction measurement metrics planning.

NOTES

Chapter 2

1. Emmett Cox, *Retail Analytics* (Hoboken, NJ: John Wiley, 2012), 19.

Chapter 5

1. Amy Cuddy, "Your Body Language Shapes Who You Are," June 2012, TED Talk, https://www.ted.com/talks/amy_cuddy_your_body_language_shapes_who _you_are?language=en.

2. Amy Cuddy, Premier Business Leadership Series, Las Vegas, Nevada, October 27–29, 2015, http://www.sas.com/en_us/events/premier-business -leadership-series/premier-business-leadership-series-2015.html#thursday.

INDEX

ACKNOWLEDGMENTS

Analytics, data, and technology are all important considerations in the transition to an analytical marketing culture, but most important are the people involved in that transformation. Vision, curiosity, and passion are the foundation for their success as analytical marketers. It was important to me that I incorporate their stories in this book. By interviewing many of the people directly involved, I was able to include relevant examples, authentic experiences, and valuable perspectives. I want to extend a huge thank you to Jennifer Chase and Matthew Fulk for being amazing partners during this journey; you are always voices of reason and your love of data provides our organization with the direction it needs.

Barbara Anthony, John Balla, Scott Batchelor, Mary Betts, Gary Catalfu, Julie Chalk, Elizabeth Creech, Cameron Dow, James Goodfellow, Gene Gsell, Linda Hester, Aaron Hill, David Macdonald, Berni Mobley, Melissa Perez, Felicia Ramsey, Scott Sellers, Shawn Skillman, Amanda Thomas, Will Waugh, Ericka Wilcher, and Patrick Xhonneux—my sincere appreciation for giving me your time, ideas, and stories and allowing me to include them in this book. Thank you for your constant inspiration.

Composing, editing, and designing this book required a terrific team that worked diligently with me over the past few years. I could not have written this book without Darren Dahl, Kelly LeVoyer, Pamela Meek, and Daniel Teachey, who have helped me bring these voices and stories to life. Thank you to Karen Day, Stacey Hamilton, Brian Jones, Felicia Ramsey, and Loretta Winstead—I am so very grateful for the support and expertise that you provided me along the way. Also, thank you to the Harvard Business Review Press team, including Gail Day, Julie Devoll, Jane Gebhart, Dave Lievens, and Melinda Merino, for bringing this book together and sharing it with the marketing world. I am fortunate to have forged so many new wonderful relationships and strengthened existing ones.

Along the way, there has been an extended team of people that have offered their services or encouragement—my thanks to Jeff Alford, Ashley Binder, Karen Campbell, Blanden Chisum, Jim Davis, Michele Eggers, Denise Lange, Angela Lipscomb, Mary Munn, Stefanie Mueller, Deb Orton, Julie Platt, Alastair Sim, Sue Talley, Nancy Wilson, and Jon Walters.

I was also very fortunate during this project to have some of our clients and my colleagues share their marketing stories and expertise from various perspectives. Emmett Cox, Brenda Hodge, Jill Dyché, Tom Davenport, Phil Brojan, Ramkumar Ravichandran, Mohammed Chaara, and James Weber—the experiences you shared gave the book substance and showcased diversity across the various fields of marketing. Thank you for your time and input. And, Tom, special thanks for being the one to spark this project.

Strength and drive come from within, but are constantly fueled by those around you at all stages of your life. For a working mom, the support system that provides that fuel is vital. My support system has always given me the guidance and confidence I need to be successful. Chris, Dylan, Cole, Jack, Michael, and Mom—thank you for your unwavering love.

ABOUT THE AUTHOR

In addition to being an authentic and passionate business leader, Adele Sweetwood is, first and foremost, a mother, wife, daughter, sister, and friend. Constantly learning from life and work experiences has enabled her to effectively strategize, problem solve, and implement change; her leadership style prioritizes collaboration, decisiveness, and communication. Leading with her head and her heart inspires creativity and accountability, building trust across her organization.

As a marketing executive with close to thirty years of accomplishments, Adele knows that marketing today is all about the customer, who is always connected and has high expectations. To lead a marketing group today, you need stamina, a sense of humor, and the occasional *Downton Abbey* marathon in order to unwind. Marketers contend with a variety of channels, devices, markets, and disruptive technologies; never before has there been such a dynamic emergence of user-generated content, social sharing, online communities, and über-informed consumers.

As Senior Vice President of Global Marketing and Shared Services at SAS, the world's leading analytics company, Adele's role is to harness all of this customer energy into strategic, high-performing marketing programs, while continually improving upon the customer experience. She is privileged to lead over 420 savvy marketers, analysts, and engagement specialists who leverage an analytical culture that enables her organization to draw customers to the SAS brand and engage them with relevant content, offers, and experiences.